SISTER HOOD PARADOX

The psychology of
female aggression at work

VANESSA VERSHAW

Testimonials

In The Sisterhood Paradox, *Vanessa Vershaw deftly confronts a hidden but critical aspect of workplace dynamics – the subtle and often unspoken challenges that women sometimes face from other women. This book is not only essential reading for those striving for gender equity but also a powerful call for solidarity and respect among women in professional spaces. Vanessa's unflinching exploration into female aggression at work provides the insight and tools needed to understand and overcome these barriers, empowering us all to foster a truly inclusive and collaborative workplace culture.*

> Dr Sandy Chong, former President, United Nations
> Association of Western Australia; Expert Network
> Member of World Economic Forum (WEF)

The issue of workplace bullying to women by women, as raised by Vanessa Vershaw in her book The Sisterhood Paradox, *is one of the most toxic, yet solvable challenges modern workplaces face – and it's not getting any better despite the financial, and other, impacts on our economy and companies. Now is the time to take action to address this by first shining a light on the issue, and then ensuring women are given the opportunity to understand the reasons behind such behaviours, how to be more self-aware, and how to deal with it when they're on the receiving end.*

> Bourby Webster, Founder, Perth Symphony Orchestra;
> Director, CAPE – Edith Cowan University

Vanessa delves into the complex dynamics of female relationships in professional environments, exploring the often-hidden issue of bullying among women at work. Through a combination of research, case studies and personal narratives, this book uncovers the psychological, social and organisational factors that contribute to this issue. The Sisterhood Paradox also offers practical strategies for individuals and organisations to foster a supportive workplace culture, empowering women to navigate and overcome the challenges of bullying. With a focus on resilience, allyship and constructive communication, this essential guide serves as a beacon of hope for those seeking to create a more harmonious and productive work environment.

Kevin Brown, CEO, St John

Thank you, Vanessa, for bringing this conversation to the forefront. For too long it has been brushed under the carpet and not recognised for what it is. Bullying of women by women in the workforce is a courageous topic because of the emotions and vulnerability that are exposed in the sharing process. Your research highlights many learning moments for all who take the time to delve into the pages of honesty, reality and truth. Congratulations for opening this Pandora's box!

Fiona Johnston, Principal, St Hilda's Anglican
School for Girls; Non-Executive Director

Vanessa's work continues to spotlight a particularly nuanced aspect of workplace bullying. While the destructive consequences of bullying on individuals and organisations are well known, the idea of women perpetrating such behaviour sits uncomfortably and challenges the ingrained belief in 'the sisterhood'. Bullying can be perpetrated by anyone, regardless of their gender. I applaud Vanessa's work for boldly addressing this complex issue and offering her fresh insights to advance gender equality and inclusivity.

Pia Turcinov, Order of Australia Recipient (2023);
Technology & Innovation Non-Executive Director

Bullying in the workplace is a destructive force, and when it happens between women, it often goes unspoken, ignored or dismissed. But this is a conversation we need to be having – openly and urgently. The impact of women bullying other women can be profound, creating toxic environments where trust, collaboration and growth are undermined. If we don't confront this issue, we allow harmful behaviours to perpetuate, leaving lasting scars on individuals and workplaces alike. Women deserve spaces where they can succeed, and failing to address this issue weakens the very foundations of equity and empowerment that we strive to build. Only by speaking openly about women bullying women can we move toward workplaces where all women uplift and support one another, fostering true collaboration and success.

Ashley McGrath, CEO, CEOs for Gender Equity

Leadership takes all forms. Vanessa Vershaw has exposed yet another example of where those who've made it may be failing those who are coming behind them.

Mark Pownall, Senior Editor, *Business News*

Exposing and addressing bullying of women in the workplace is crucial for achieving gender equity; only by dismantling these barriers can we create an environment where all voices are heard and valued equally. Vanessa Vershaw courageously tackles this issue head on, asking challenging questions and getting to the core of this issue, revealing truths and real-life stories we cannot ignore, leaving us with only one choice: we must act now, each and every one of us, to be the change we need to see.

Rabia Siddique, International Humanitarian and Human Rights Lawyer; Best-selling Author, *Courage Under Fire*

Vanessa Vershaw asks us to look inward and consider what's at the heart of female–female bullying: an issue that's easily ignored, often denied and yet lingers with devastating impacts on people and workplaces. Not an easy read, but an awkward conversation we need to have – still. If you've ever felt the hunger-like pangs of scarcity, delivered or been on the receiving end of self-doubt-inducing exclusion – you need this book. Let's face it: we all need this book.

Carmen Braidwood, Media Trainer, Presenter and Speaker

Why are we not making material progress in terms of gender diversity and equity? While central to progress is the achievement of a social and economic culture of positive masculinity, we must also leverage change in how women support women in the workplace and beyond. I highly recommend The Sisterhood Paradox *as essential reading as we seek to address and achieve gender equity. Vanessa's perspective and challenge is insightful and inspiring, and advances the spirit of collaboration, coaching and care to, for and from women as we change our world together.*

Barry Bloch, Global Partner Board &
Executive Leadership, Gerard Daniels

Vanessa is bravely addressing the elephant in the room, which is that, in many cases, it is women not men who are holding back gender equality in the workplace. It is easier to blame the patriarchy and scream sexism than to hold a mirror up and acknowledge that women bullying women is a huge barrier to our progression. I hope this book acts as a trigger for all female leaders to reflect on their own behaviour at work.

Kristen Turnbull, Founding Director, CoreData

This is an important book for women who are being bullied and for organisational leaders who want to make a difference. If you are a woman bullied or suppressed by someone else, this book is an essential resource for explaining the probable reasons for the asocial behaviour inflicted on you and providing ideas on what you can do about it. For organisational leaders, the book provides a call to action for knowing what to watch for, understanding the trauma that bullying can cause and setting the standards you are prepared to tolerate and not tolerate.

Andrew O'Keeffe, author, *Hardwired Humans* and *The Boss*

Women bullying women in the workplace is an organisational sickness that must be cured. This book shines a spotlight on the problem, educates through examples, and gives both women and men the tools they need to fix it. This is a must-read for everyone is all areas of business.

Darcy Nybo, author and founder of Artistic Warrior Publishing (Canada)

Workplace bullying increases the risk of depression, anxiety, chronic stress and suicidal thoughts and behaviours. This book has helped several of my female patients make sense of their suicidal ideation and, most importantly, understand that they are not alone, offering strategies and tips for handling toxic bullies. It's imperative to keep the conversation going and to keep encouraging each other to speak up.

Donna Stambulich, Clinical Psychology Director, Re-code Psychology Centre

Vanessa Vershaw is a true trailblazer, taking to another level topics that are often swept under the carpet. She is shining a light on the crucial topic of women bullying women, where to date the responsibility for these actions has mostly been attributed to the men's world. A must-read for women and men of all ages.

Barbara McNaught, host and producer, *Hello Darlink!* talk show

Thank you, Vanessa, for making this important work a priority. Your continued focus on making life better for the sisterhood is more important than ever. Your use of stories and case studies to articulate the issue, coupled with tools to help employees and employers, is outstanding.

Paula Rogers, CEO, Committee for Perth

Also by Vanessa Vershaw

Unreasonable ambition helps people do extraordinary things.

Vanessa Vershaw's compelling debut, *Unreasonable Ambition*, is a call for courageous leadership in an era of unprecedented complexity. Drawing on her extensive experience as a psychologist, transformation strategist and global adviser to some of the world's most influential organisations, Vanessa challenges conventional thinking and lays out a path for a radical shift in how we lead, grow and define success.

Blending sharp insight with practical application, *Unreasonable Ambition* encourages leaders to embrace discomfort, cultivate personal mastery and step beyond the status quo. It is a book for those who believe that bold, human-centred leadership is not only possible but essential – and who are ready to make that leap.

This provocative and empowering book positions Vanessa as a vital voice in the conversation on leadership, culture and change.

*This book is dedicated to our daughters
Allegra Lia and Marilou Catherine, and all the
cherished girls and beloved women in your lives.*

*May it provide them with the conviction
to stand up for their beliefs, the courage to
be trailblazers, the wisdom to get ahead
and the freedom to shine brightly.*

Thank you
for reading my
book Rodger
I hope you
enjoy it

Wesham

*Sisters may drive you crazy, get into your stuff,
and irritate you. However, if anyone else dares say
so, a sister will defend you to the death.*

Unknown

Acknowledgements

To do something that terrifies you requires the support of a million souls behind you to ensure that the many arrows fired in your back bounce off so that you can keep going.

This release of this fully revised edition would not have been possible without the honesty and bravery of so many women and men who have encouraged the raw unveiling of a topic that the world needs to talk about. I am so grateful for all your help and am emboldened to keep going on the road less travelled.

Thank you to my fabulous husband for talking me out of my self-doubt every day and my parents Penelope and Robert for their unwavering belief in me.

Thank you to the amazing duo of Charlotte Duff from Publish Central and Megan McCracken for their incredible reviewing and editing skills.

To my publisher Michael Hanrahan and his team including my ever-gracious book designer Julia Kuris for keeping me on track.

To my coach Andrew Griffiths for his limitless wisdom pushing me forward and Amy Henderson for her incredible research eyes.

To my friends Stephen Quantrill for always backing me, Sara Lord for being my soul sister and Kerrie Allen my much-treasured 'work wife' and teammate.

To my co-writer Jean-François Ducharme, we started this together my friend and I will love you always for saying YES.

And finally, to my miracle children Allegra and Noah – you are my greatest source of inspiration and make me better as a human. Thank you for choosing me to be your mother.

First published in 2025 by Vanessa Vershaw

A Cataloguing-in-Publication entry is available for this book from the
National Library of Australia

ISBN: 978-1-923225-74-9

Printed in Australia by Pegasus
Project management and text design by Publish Central
Cover design by Julia Kuris

Disclaimer
The material in this publication is of the nature of general comment only and
does not represent professional advice. It is not intended to provide specific
guidance for particular circumstances, and it should not be relied on as the
basis for any decision to take action or not take action on any matter which
it covers. Readers should obtain professional advice where appropriate, before
making any such decision. To the maximum extent permitted by law, the
author and associated entities and publisher disclaim all responsibility and
liability to any person, arising directly or indirectly from any person taking or
not taking action based on the information in this publication.

While this book was inspired by true events, many of the names have been
changed to protect the guilty and the innocent.

Contents

Why the world needs this updated edition now

The Asia–Pacific is a region with great potential in economic terms; a growing, young and vibrant part of the world where women have been playing important roles for centuries. Yet, their contributions have not been recognised as they should. So let us recognise the various challenges women face around the world and try to do our best to support them through experience sharing, raising awareness and recognising the role women play in their countries' development.

Pimchanok Pitfield, World Trade Organization
Ambassador for Thailand, World Women Foundation,
APAC Equality Moonshot, Davos, January 2025

Earlier this year, I found myself having a surreal experience sitting on a stage in Davos, Switzerland, representing the APAC region at the 2025 World Woman Foundation, talking about advancing gender equality. The panel event I was invited to speak on was held literally at the top of a mountain, as part of a side event to the Annual General Meeting of the World Economic Forum (WEF).[1]

I was one of three panellists (and the only Australian invited to speak) on the APAC Equality Moonshot, and was asked to speak about Australia's progress in the diversity, equality and inclusion (DEI) space – and I was feeling the weight of it because of what I knew.

Sitting next to me on the panel were two women representing some broad perspectives – from the World Trade Organization's (WTO) Ambassador for Thailand, Pimchanok Pitfield, singing the praises of her government increasing the placement of women in leadership roles by 85 per cent, and Director of the WTO Accessions Division, Maika Oshikawa, sharing her story of an inability to return to her home country (Japan) because of a lack of progress. Our moderator was the impressive Dr Sandy Chong, Singaporean entrepreneur and sustainability expert deftly carving her niche for Asian women in international business – a wonderful success story.

In the back of my mind, I was aware that I was about to publish a book that would challenge existing notions of the issues negatively affecting the psychological wellbeing of young girls and holding professional women back from significant moves ahead. I was also mindful of the state of play for women back home and managing my nerves as I searched for the words to represent my country in a way that balanced politics, sensitivities and raw truth – without distancing the 300 attendees in the room and the thousands who were tuning in on the livestream.

But the theme for the Davos event was to be ambitious, brave and bold – and so I was. I shared what I knew – that not only has the progress for women slowed down to a trickle, and even stopped in some parts of the world, but also (much as it might be a bitter pill to swallow) women have some part to play in this lack of progress. The way some women act in the workplace – from failing to lift other women to active aggression and bullying – is holding other women back and perpetuating cultural stereotypes about women. Most of us are still in denial about how bad this behaviour is – and that's what we need to talk about.

With that, I'm now doubling up on my courage and about to reveal some disheartening truths so you understand why I felt so compelled to release this new edition to the world right now.

The inconvenient truth

We have entered an unpredictable new world in our press for progress – a world that is barely recognisable from ten years ago (around when the first edition of this book was released), and more complex to navigate than ever before. The Earth around us is morphing and stretching with each new extreme challenge and existential threat, but as a society we have not changed enough to run at pace with its rapid transformation.

Our reality is still a place where men and women are not treated with respect and valued equally.

But you would be forgiven for thinking otherwise. Indeed, we have been inundated with a frenzy of activity suggesting the opposite. A rise in the launching of women-only associations, conferences and networking events, along with media spotlights and talks, has masked the truth.

Our reality is still a place where men and women are not treated with respect and valued equally.

If you were to ask most people how far we've come with gender equality, they'd probably tell you about the great strides we have made in creating a world that is fairer for women everywhere. They might share with you what they see in their mind's eye – a line stretching around the block of bold and determined women, heads held high as they march their way into power, tipping the scale with every step they take.

A wonderful dream and necessary evolution that the world is demanding from us in the way we live, work and relate to one another – if we want to be around for the next 100 years. And it's an awe-inspiring vision.

Unfortunately, this vision is still at odds with our reality. We have not made significant progress advancing women at work – and, in many ways, we've gone backwards. Women often remain spectators in the world of work, relegated to the sidelines and absent from key decision-making groups. To illustrate this, international data reveals that the leadership gender gap has widened. Globally, every year since 2016, we have seen a 1 per cent increase in the hiring rate of women into leadership positions. Since the COVID-19 pandemic, however, the representation of senior women has not only lost momentum but also started to decline – sending us backwards since 2021.[2]

Women often remain spectators in the world of work, relegated to the sidelines and absent from key decision-making groups.

Jaw to the floor.

And Australia it seems is in state of delusion – or what well-known journalist Catherine Fox refers to as 'over optimism'[3] (I think she's being kind!) – as to the progress we have made. Findings showcase in iridescent neon technicolour the widely held view that we have taken big steps forward, more than we really have – 59 per cent of Australian respondents in a 2023 survey on gender attitudes, for example, believe that we have pretty much hit gender equality or are already there.[4]

The truth is the threat to gender equality has never been more real than right now, and we are losing the battle.

It's clear that the lack of movement on this front is complex and multifaceted to unravel – and it's also understandable how our judgement may have become skewed when looking through the lens of the highly publicised window dressing (such as well-marketed women's programs, focus on recruitment targets and quotas, mandated diversity initiatives and ergonomically friendly breastfeeding rooms).

These 'advancements' are served up to us daily to give the veneer of momentum and mask the inconvenience of bad news. In the midst of all this, many are reportedly withering on the vine from 'diversity fatigue' and don't want to hear about it anymore.[5]

Life has also become more complex to decipher, with our sight blurred by the COVID-19 fog and rise of perceived female tokenism, taking us away from what was a positive and inclusive feminist agenda based on merit. The rise of the #MeToo movement, cancel culture, introduction of gender pronouns, unregulated media industry, increase in reported domestic violence cases and much-needed critical reforms in our sexual harassment and anti-discrimination laws – all worthy objects of our attention – have also taken the focus off the goal of equal opportunity, giving the impression that we are done and dusted in this area – which couldn't be further from the truth.

Further evidence suggests that taking our eye off the gender equality prize has also been compounded by the resentment and very real backlash we're facing from the 'brotherhood'. This backlash threatens gender targets and blocks the push for greater diversity, with some of the reasons cited being annoyance from hearing about gender equality so frequently, fear of navigating the possibility of a new world order and a desire to keep things exactly as they are. Some also argue that men aren't comfortable talking about gender equality because they feel they have not been invited into the conversation, and so feel excluded and less likely to become advocates.[6]

As an example of this, Megan McCracken, award-winning gender advocate[7], shared a conversation she had in a board meeting with a gentleman who said the following:

Look, there is something that men will never tell you and that is that many of them – particularly aged 30 to 50 – genuinely fear that the advancement of women in the workplace will disadvantage them and that they will lose their jobs. While this fear exists, progress will be slow.[8]

A recent report from Chief Executive Women (CEW), *Senior Executive Census 2024*, aptly subtitled 'Keeping Score of a Losing Game', showcases the rippling impact of this unsettling perspective – the eight years of data in the report displays how change in Australia has ground to a halt and is even 'sliding backwards' in some areas of gender equality for the first time since the pandemic. For example, the CEW survey highlighted only one in eight CEO appointments were women, compared with one in four in 2023.[9]

The lesser-known obstacle holding women back

Along with the perception gender equality has already been achieved in many workplaces and the backlash from men on pushing for further advancements, another obstacle is also at play – one that is still considered by many to be a hidden but critical aspect of workplace dynamics that is holding women back at work and stopping us experiencing change at the rate it is needed. This aspect has grown and evolved in the workplace, even if our numbers have not.

I'm talking here about the paradox of the sisterhood, and how the way some women treat other women in the workplace has created an additional barrier to the advancement of women – the sisterhood ceiling. This is the subtle and often unspoken challenges caused by women mistreating each other at work, blocking their progress, and even actively targeting their removal from the race. These behaviours are counterproductive to the bigger game we need to win for all women everywhere – and no-one is talking about them.

And it's still alive and well.

These are the words of a well-known Australian CEO of a creative economy business and former public government official who (shuddering as she recalled her experience) told me:

In my experience, sometimes certain women groups or committees appear to operate as a sort of bitch mafia. They add no value. It's just mean girls. I haven't let the bitches get me down, but it does make you think, how many women have been brought down by other women or have not met or achieved their potential because of other women?

I first kick-started the conversation in 2016 with the Canadian release of *Bitch Fight: Put an End to Women Bullying Women in the Workplace*, co-authored with renowned clinical psychologist Dr Jean-François Ducharme – who was a collaborator with me on the earlier edition and brought important balance to the conversation. *Bitch Fight* was written with the intent to raise awareness on a toxic and pervasive phenomenon confronting women at work. Leading up to writing the book, a few things were going on that rocked our world. In our coaching and therapy business, Jean-François and I had seen an increase in the number of female clients who were grappling with significant mental health challenges after being mistreated or bullied by other women at work. We even lost a patient to suicide.

As psychologists, we knew of the strong correlation between rapid mental health deterioration and bullying, with some countries showing that at least half of reported suicides are linked to bullying. While it's difficult to be precise on the numbers, when we published *Bitch Fight*, our research showed that women are 30 per cent more likely to experience bullying at work than men – but when women bully, they target women 70 per cent of the time.[10] We also knew that the psychological impact of women facing aggression from or being bullied by other women was far more psychologically damaging, often leading to suicide or death.

Bitch Fight was written to provide a much-needed psychological deep dive into a lesser-known threat to female advancement that was grossly misunderstood (most people don't know how to spot the difference between bad behaviour and more severe bullying) and under-investigated in the research. We provided a detailed real-life example of coaching one of our executive clients through her CEO journey amid relentless female rivalry and aggression. We also provided well-tested psychological tools and techniques to help readers better navigate the impact of what can be tricky and complex dynamics.

But here's the conundrum. Almost a decade on, we are no further along in understanding the psychology of female aggression toward other women and bullying in today's workplace. (They are still called out as one and the same, for example!) Ironically, just as our digital world is advancing at warp speed, so too are the bullying tactics – which have achieved scale, becoming more sophisticated with broader reach. As an example, what were once acts of one-on-one psychological harassment, bad behaviours or targeted violence have extended to include mobbing[11] (where a perpetrator recruits others to do their dirty work without it sticking to them).

> *Ironically, just as our digital world is advancing at warp speed, so too are the bullying tactics.*

The impact of bullying behaviours has also become more widespread due to the manic increase in incidents of trolling[12] and cyberbullying[13], with a recent study showcasing that Australian school children are among the most bullied in the world, behind only Latvia[14].

This disturbing increase in both frequency and methods of bullying highlights it's time for us to take the blinkers off and find out more about the issues affecting overall workplace health and wellbeing – not to mention the impact on women, who are 93 per cent more susceptible to occupational health concerns such as burnout and extreme stress than men[15], and less likely to take time off due to mental health concerns.

We're also paying a hefty price for these impacts. As an example, in 2001 the Australian Productivity Commission estimated that workplace bullying was costing the Australian economy between $6 billion and $36 billion every year, based on reported cases. Updating that figure more than 20 years on translates to a (conservative) estimated annual cost to the economy of $10 to $60 billion. However, researchers also argue this figure doesn't take into account additional 'hidden' costs of workplace bully.[16]

But there's more to this conversation we need to explore.

From glass to sisterhood ceiling

Everyone has heard of the 'glass ceiling' – the systemic invisible barrier preventing women from being promoted into senior level leadership roles and stopping the progress of women. Researchers are now identifying an additional layer in the invisible ceilings hampering a female's climb up the workplace ladder: a 'sisterhood ceiling' that is created by women actively preventing women from progressing in their careers.

And here is why this is worthy of deeper scrutiny – the views on whether it's a real thing or not are polarised. Don't get me wrong, no-one denies that women holding back other women occurs, but disagreement exists as to how bad it really is and how often it is happening. (In general, it's only the women who have experienced it who really feel the pain of it!) Further, no-one really wants to talk about it – whether they have been a target or not.

Of course, the widely held perception is that women don't really help each other at work, preferring to 'tear each other down and claw their way into the top jobs'. Even Dr Susan Maushart, well-respected author of *The Mask of Motherhood* and *Wifework*, a columnist for the *Weekend Australian Magazine* and a research associate at Curtin University in Western Australia, was quoted at a Women in Media conference as saying, 'You don't need to worry about women getting to the top. Women are like a basket of crabs – they just pull each other down'.

Jamila Rizvi, columnist at *The Sydney Morning Herald*, shares this view. In her article 'Yes, sometimes women are sexist too. Let's look a little deeper', she shares her experiences working with organisations to advance gender equality – and her uncovering of a prevailing belief that the problem is not that sexism exists, nor how men treat women; it's how women treat women at work.

And then there's highly respected feminist Catherine Fox, mentioned earlier. She says that the existence of so many support groups for women provides evidence of a trend that is 'at odds with the enduring Queen Bee clichés and cultural mean girls tropes suggesting women are particularly prone to stabbing each other in the back'.[17]

So where are we really?

Here's what we do know for sure. While it may be harder to recognise in some cases, female bullies targeting other women is still happening. It starts early, and it is still an issue we are not facing.

Take Charlotte O'Brien, the 12-year-old student from Santa Sabina College in Strathfield in Sydney's Inner West who took her own life in September 2024 after allegedly being cyberbullied by girls who still attend her school. She wrote a note mentioning the bullying she received. Her parents claimed the school investigated the allegations and the girls denied it.

And this is a case we know about.

It also seems that schoolyard antics are following us into workplaces worldwide.

Take a look at the numbers.

In a 2017 survey, the US Workplace Bullying Institute found that when women bully, they bully other women up to 80 per cent of the time. A further study from the University of Arizona showed that women who report to women experience a greater frequency of bullying, abuse and job sabotage.[18]

More current US-based data from 2024 shows that women are still bullying women at twice the rate they bully men. Specifically, 71 per cent of bullies are males, of whom 55 per cent target males and 45 per cent target females. In contrast, of the 29 per cent of women who bully others, 67 per cent target females and 33 per cent target males.[19]

In Australia, however, we are flying blind with little data to go on except to claim that violence remains a significant barrier to gender equality, with current data listing Australia and New Zealand as the worst global region for workplace violence and harassment.[20]

Whichever way you slice it, the data is screaming at us to take a more meaningful look at bullying and women – if we want to build positive learning environments and supportive workplace cultures where women are empowered and flourish.

The Sisterhood Paradox is a new edition of *Bitch Fight*, revised and updated almost ten years on to reflect how the modern-day workplace has evolved and to shine the light on the continued incidence of female aggression and bullying as counterproductive to achieving more ambitious goals such as women having equal rights in our labour economy and progressing up the food chain at work.

The need for us to solve what is undoubtedly an increasingly complex challenge of our time cannot be underestimated – especially since 'continued economic growth will rely on organisations, including political organisations, harnessing the other 50 per cent of the population in a meaningful way'[21] and dismantling rigid gender norms, which would add circa $128 billion annually to the Australian economy.[22]

So, it makes business sense as well.

The inspiration for the revised and updated edition

Personally, and professionally, the decision to release this updated edition has been terrifying for me. (In truth, it would have been safer for me to leave it behind me to gather dust and maintain a coveted place in my memoirs!)

Terrifying because of the risks associated with talking about a topic that naturally attracts public judgement and the possibility of exclusion for those who mention it.

Terrifying because of those who believe that raising this issue may thwart the broader goals of gender equality at work.

Terrifying because this may be seen by some as typecasting women as innately bitchy, less capable and ineffective as leaders.

This is not my intention.

The reality is we are far from done with gender equality, and for things to change, we must change.

The purpose of this book is to issue a call to action to get the discussion going on the under-examined threat of female aggression and bullying in the workplace. Through examining this threat more closely, we have the potential to create awareness about the importance of allyship in building more positive environments for us all to flourish.

At Davos, despite my trepidation, the response to my sharing some of the findings and arguments outlined in this book was overwhelming, with many women in the room thanking me for my bravery in addressing the 'elephant in the room' that 'we cannot avoid tackling any longer'.

Dealing with female bullying could very well be the lever we have yet to pull to accelerate the progress we need.

This book is also a request to all advocates for gender equality to commit to leaving no stone unturned in our quest to get a forceful swing of the pendulum in our favour. Dealing with female bullying could very well be the lever we have yet to pull to accelerate the progress we need.

In the pages that follow, I delve deeper into the topic, outlining the psychological drivers and counter-productive impacts of female aggression and bullying at work. I bring together current research and my expertise as an organisational psychologist and business coach, working with over 70 women who have experienced workplace bullying from other women. Between 2015 and 2024 I facilitated roundtables with female business leaders and interviews with over 85 global C-suite leaders – men and women from a broad range of roles and industry sectors – to gather their perspectives on what they think is going on.[23]

Through this exploration, you will gain a more comprehensive understanding of the complex dynamics at play, and develop practical, targeted and effective strategies to address the toxic dynamics that might be hindering your ability to build and enjoy harmonious and productive modern-day workplaces where all women can thrive.

An unreasonably ambitious vision for an empowered future

As I reflect on the journey that brought me here, I am filled with immense gratitude for the courageous women who entrusted me with their stories, and I honour their request for anonymity. Each shared experience, laden with tears and fears for the future, ignited a spark of hope in me. Your belief in the light on the horizon has inspired this new edition.

Imagine a world where everyone and every voice is not just heard but celebrated, where collaboration, respect, allyship and inclusion are the foundation of our workplaces.

It is my fervent hope that this book serves as a catalyst for action, igniting a movement towards an empowered future for generations yet to come.

Imagine a world where everyone and every voice is not just heard but celebrated, where collaboration, respect, allyship and inclusion are the foundation of our workplaces.

To all women, let's write a new story so powerful that it changes the world, together.

Now be unreasonably ambitious and get ready as I begin by sharing my own experiences and the fire that ignited this book.

Behind closed doors

There's a special place in hell reserved for women who don't help other women

Madeleine Albright, former US Secretary of State

It's January 2008 and I'm in Boston. Temperatures are arctic and the snow has turned into icy rain. No matter which direction I turn outside, I get a frigid slap in the face. By 9 am that morning, I had run five kilometres on an indoor treadmill, watched CNN, taken a ride in a Toronto taxi, and endured three tasteless cappuccinos at the airport while awaiting my flight. Now I was in Boston in the boardroom on the top floor of a well-known American bank. I was there to meet with the executive team and talk them into spending big bucks. I planned to show them how to do a better job of harnessing the potential in their organisation and release their next generation of leaders. That's one of the joys of believing you are Wonder Woman. You push yourself so hard that you start to believe you're infallible. You're so controlled and over-prepared that nothing can ever go wrong.

Back to the boardroom. The 180-degree views of Boston Harbor and the Atlantic Ocean are spectacular. I secretly congratulate myself. I know I've got this gig in the bag. As a senior executive of a well-known human capital company, I've been schmoozing this mob for months. Today is the day I'm going to seal the deal. I'd already planned my celebration. Since I was going to be spending so much time in Boston, I'd decided after they'd signed off on the contract,

I'd treat myself and buy a season's pass to catch Red Sox games at Fenway Park. I was really pumped.

Nothing could have been further from reality. You see, back at my head office was an operations manager called Tiffany who had delusions of grandeur – and was secretly plotting my demise. Tiffany had made her way into a professional position by having razor-sharp street smarts and a burning hunger to succeed. It amazed me how in an elitist organisation like ours, where educational pedigree was everything, she had even made it through the door.

Tiffany was charged with preparing the sales materials for the session, which included setting up the video-conferencing technology. I'd decided not to show them the usual PowerPoint slides. Instead, we were going to wow our Boston clients with interactive charts, live video streaming and the benefit of Tiffany's insights around online talent assessment systems.

In the boardroom, I'm juiced and ready. I take my position at the head of the table, poised and ready for the show. I would dazzle them with my showmanship and talk them through the glossy information packs. Being an infotainer is a critical skill to master when you're a human capital consultant. You need to be memorable, and I'm determined not to leave the meeting empty handed.

As the executive team members open their packs, I realise something is very wrong. I'm met with a succession of confused looks as their team stare at me. I pick one of the packs up to discover it's empty!

I decide not to let it get to me because I am the queen of cool. I'm the one who stays calm under pressure. I know I can handle this. I've had to wing it many times before; this would be no different. I'll use the whiteboard. I can do this. I'm feeling rather smug about my over-preparedness and my impressive skills of improvisation. I will triumph and save the day.

Everyone settles and Tiffany appears on the big screen. I don't let my hostility show. I'll deal with her later. Suddenly we hear a child's scream. Tiffany runs off camera saying something about her son falling and cracking his head open. Then the screen goes blank.

Silence.

I never saw that executive team again.

The next two months went from bad to worse. Losing that opportunity threw my competence into question. Unbeknown to me, Tiffany had been undermining me for months, taking advantage of my absences as I travelled around the country. She had cast doubt on my leadership competence to secure her position as next in line. She'd gifted tickets to a Toronto Raptors game to my executive assistant, gotten mighty chummy with the CFO, and fudged my sales pipeline. When the shit hit the fan, it landed all over me.

Tiffany's edge was to present herself as the underdog trying to make a go of it in a world she wanted so desperately to be part of. I provided a stark contrast to Tiffany and fit all the traditional criteria to make it. To her, I had a target on my back that flashed like strobe lights at a disco.

The ending was textbook. I grew weary of dodging the heavy artillery fire that came my way daily. Feeling like I was fighting a battle I couldn't win, I left the company. My faith in my boss and what he stood for had taken a nosedive. I fired the organisation and 'divorced' my famous boss.

I learned some big life lessons from that time of my life. As for regrets, I do have one. I regret I didn't let Tiffany go when I had the chance. My boss had given me the opportunity after her other sneaky moves – such as overriding my authority on key business decisions in my absence and hurling foul-mouthed abuse at other team members in public view – became known. At the time, I flat-out turned him down.

To be honest, I know that I had been more concerned about playing the nice-girl card than I was about getting results. I was guilty of what former Meta Platforms and Facebook COO Sheryl Sandberg describes as the curse we women have of trying to be liked at all costs, even at our own expense. My decision to be nice and my fear of the dreaded 'bitch' label led to me resigning and saying goodbye to the corner office (and the great view!).

My story is not unusual. As a high-performance coach and workplace psychologist, I have now coached countless male and female leaders who have shared similar tales involving powerful, destructive women, often with worse outcomes.

What is important, though, is that whether my clients have been in altercations themselves or have witnessed others having the experience, the deleterious psychological impact often runs deep and can last a lifetime.

The good news for me is that my fall from grace was short lived. Yes, the bullying experience stung, but it also presented a formidable professional growth opportunity. I realised how much our strong need for approval as women can limit our potential.

> *Women will often significantly diminish their own sphere of influence by focusing on maintaining relationships at the expense of getting results.*

Women will often significantly diminish their own sphere of influence by focusing on maintaining relationships at the expense of getting results. Research shows we like to be seen as agreeable, caring, nurturing and collegial.[24] So how do we as women stop our natural need for keeping the peace at all costs? We can start by quitting our nauseating apologising, tossing out some of the tact and constructively confronting the bullies in our lives.

Elizabeth Gilbert, author of the popular novel *Eat, Pray, Love*, sums up the essence of this approach – and this book – so well with the following:

> *The women whom I love and admire for their grace and strength did not get that way because shit worked out. They got that way because shit went wrong, and they handled it. They handled it in a thousand*

different ways, on a thousand different days, but they handled it. Those women are my superheroes.

Since releasing the first edition of this book in 2016, I have been inundated by countless requests from men to include their experiences being bullied by women at work. In professions where females outnumber males, such as nursing, males are more likely to be bullied than females.[25] While this is not the focus for this book, it adds weight to the argument that it is not gender that matters as much as the power imbalance that exists between genders. As such, females are just as likely to be bullies compared to males, particularly when they are empowered to do so. Field data reveals that while female to male bullying is not as a common an occurrence overall as women to women – as mentioned, figures from the US show 67 per cent of female bullies target females while 33 per cent target males – it is equally as traumatic and worthy of broader discussion.

As well as uncovering the nature of female bullying, this book is also an exploration of how people who have overcome workplace bullying have risen stronger after their experiences. They are my inspiration for writing this book. I hope that sharing their stories will empower others to take back control of their careers and create the life they want.

Introduction

Whack! Crack! Thud!

Did you hear that sound? It happened again. Another woman just cracked her head on that impenetrable concrete ceiling. Her head is pounding and throbs with a dull ache. It sucks to be her.

But who put the ceiling there?

Contrary to popular belief, it's not just men who build it. Women mistreating their sisters in business are also responsible for actively blocking other women's rise up the corporate ladder. The 'sisterhood ceiling', as it's been called, is another key contributor to the ongoing battle for women to achieve equality in the workplace – and it ain't pretty.

The evidence on what this looks like is clear. As mentioned, a 2024 report published by the US Workplace Bullying Institute highlighted that females still are more likely to bully other females – targeting women in 67 per cent of cases, and men in 33 per cent.[26] What has also been uncovered is that as women have risen into leadership positions, the rate of women being bullied at work has also increased. While solid data on who is doing the bullying is unclear, this is worthy of a mention.

As a high-performance coach and organisational psychologist, I have witnessed a wide range of workplace crimes. But seeing successful professional women behave badly towards other women at work remains one of the more disturbing displays of corrosive behaviour I have ever witnessed – probably because it's so unexpected and not so easy to detect. Ask most women how they feel after being on the receiving end of female bullying, and the words they typically use are 'side swiped', 'blindsided' or 'sucker punched' – it was so completely unexpected they just didn't see it coming. Women bullying their female colleagues is also on the rise in the modern-day workplace, alongside other forms of bullying and workplace violence. Collectively, these are believed to be major sources of competitive disadvantage for organisations worldwide, costing Australian businesses an estimated $30 billion per year.[27]

This begs the question: how is it that with the reported incidence of women sabotaging other women at work being so high, it remains a phenomenon cloaked in silence? Why is no-one talking about it?

> *Quite simply, female bullying is a subject that remains taboo and just isn't given any airtime.*

Based on my and Jean-François's work with females who have been targets of female aggression, I've come up with five reasons:

1. Most people don't really understand what female-to-female bullying looks like.
2. They are too scared to talk about it.
3. They don't know what to do about it.
4. It's considered a taboo topic.
5. All of the above.

Quite simply, female bullying is a subject that remains taboo and just isn't given any airtime.

What has confounded a solid understanding of female aggression in all its permutations is that most of us don't really know how to call it out – because it's not obvious.

The 'weapons of choice' between genders are also usually different, with males often preferring a more direct approach (that is, they tend to call it and 'duke' it out) and females often using more covert tactics (such as operating in secrecy, discrediting other women, fat and slut shaming, remarks veiled in double entendre, tall poppy takedowns and passive aggressive attacks).[28] That's what makes female bullying behaviour so hard to distinguish. Dr Juliet Bourke, professor at the University of New South Wales and former Partner in Human Capital at Deloitte, describes this wonderfully when she says, 'the indirect approach is harder to deal with, like sand through your fingers'.

And yet with each closed mouth and awkward silence, the issue of women mistreating other women at work remains an invisible threat that can ruin careers, cause organisational decline and leave broken people in its wake.[29]

I wrote this book for all those whose lives have been turned upside down by bullying, in the spirit of providing them hope. In the following chapters, I provide an understanding of the what, the how and the why, and share strategies and insights into combating this behaviour. My aim overall is to help you deal with the bullies at work who may be making your life hell or preventing you from having the job and career that you want and deserve.

About this book

This is a book primarily about female aggression, hostility and bullying in the workplace. I also cover off on those with more untreatable conditions, including female narcissists and psychopaths, just to make sure all the bases are covered. My goal is to describe the different types of bullies from all angles, help you build some coping skills if you have gone or are going through it, and try to prevent its future occurrence. Learning how to navigate this successfully will not only set you up for a more successful career but also help pave the way for an equal future for us all, with more women at the helm making decisions that make a difference.

Part I of this book outlines a specific leadership story – Kathryn's story. Being able to connect with a real person, to learn from her experiences, and draw meaning and life lessons from a real situation makes the research more tangible and the tools easier to apply.

Kathryn's story is the tale of a talented and successful executive who takes a stab at the CEO position in her company. This story reveals the corruption and tactics of multiple players in her organisation who try to stop her from getting the job. Inspired by true events, Kathryn's story illustrates what can really happen when a woman makes a play for the top job in a traditionally male-dominated family enterprise. The names of all characters (except for myself and Jean-François) and the companies in question have been changed to maintain our oath of confidentiality.

As I take you on her journey, I also include in-time coaching insights from myself and Jean-François. Between us, we have over 40 years of experience as executive coaches, and workplace and clinical psychologists working with ASX-20 and Fortune 100 organisations globally. You'll get to be in the room, hearing the inner workings of a coach's mind, finding out what is said and done during intimate coaching sessions. You will also get a behind-closed-door view of the 'A-ha' moments that came to light, learn how pitfalls are overcome, and watch leaders evolving in real time. And you'll be given the critical information you need to spot the difference between bullies and workplace psychopaths – and know how to avoid their traps.

In the chapters in part II, I draw on real-life client stories standing alongside over 1000 leaders in over 20 countries across 50+ industry sectors to provide solutions on how to deal with situations involving women bullies at work. Collaborating with Jean-François, I share our views and guidance along the way to equip you with the skills to manage these situations and come out on top.

The phenomenon of women mistreating and bullying women at work must be put into context. When you understand what's really going on, you can sharpen your skills and know how to manage the situation – and how to prevent yourself going down with it.

Chapter 17, 'Men rule the world, still', outlines how far women have progressed – and how far away they still are from their destination.

To believe that women have truly made great strides toward equality is akin to believing in Father Christmas and the Easter Bunny. I know this is sounding a touch cynical; however, the data supports my positioning on how far we have come – and the areas in which we've gone backwards – despite all the attention gender equality has been given. This chapter provides the brutal facts on the current state of play and sets the stage for understanding how much women are held back by organisational systems and traditional beliefs.

In chapter 18, 'It's (still) all about sex', I turn things upside down and take on the quest of understanding the root of women-on-women fighting. This takes us back to the beginning of time – and the explanation I outline might not be what you expect. I tackle the issue from the ground up and discuss how women have the power to better manage their biases toward other women and halt an irresistible urge to some downright mean behaviours. I also run through how tactics have evolved over the last 10 years (since the first edition of this book) to become more sophisticated and sinister.

Next up is chapter 19, 'A bully by any other name', where I examine the attitudes to workplace female bullying and find out why it remains taboo. The research uncovers deep resistance from leaders to openly talking about female bullying, while acknowledging the devastating impact it has on so many lives. At the same time, I debunk some persistent myths about regular garden-variety 'mean girls', and the more insidious bullying behaviours. Getting caught up in bullying is a slippery slope to navigate. I outline the type of fertile soil that can favour the emergence of the 'queen bee', and show you how to deal with the difficult people at work. The chapter closes with a lesson in how to move on from a bully's attack that is worth meditating over. In chapter 20, I compare your standard mean girl, bully and psychopath at work. Each persona requires a specific handling strategy to make it out unscathed.

In chapter 21, 'Gender blind and deaf', I look at female aggression from a male perspective. You may be surprised by how unaware men are of women-on-women bullying in the workplace. In this chapter,

I run through how male responses change when they have a daughter, sister or wife on the receiving end of bullying. Their answers are quite illuminating and help us make sense of how to work together better.

It would be remiss of me not to include some tips and guidelines to help you understand whether you are a potential target or not. The reality is that at some point in their careers, most people will be confronted by a bully at work. You can't avoid them, and I don't want you to. Dodging this issue will leave you worse off, as you either leave the organisation or become a victim – not an intelligent career strategy. I outline some better strategies in chapter 22, 'Are you a target?' And in chapter 23, 'Stop being so bloody nice', I explore some of the ingrained behaviours and social conditioning that can hold women back from stepping into their full potential – and how to overcome them.

To wrap things up, I want to leave you feeling confident, ready to manage female workplace aggression and overthrow the bullies at work, and boost the quality of your working life. In chapter 24, 'Let's bake a new pie', I provide a vision of what's possible, while chapter 25, 'Stop talking and start walking', outlines how you can accelerate your productivity and leadership effectiveness in ways that are both achievable and sustainable. At a systems level, I also delve into some key strategies to build competitive advantage for both you and the company you work for. Lastly, I finish up in chapter 26, 'Creating a new tomorrow', with some words of inspiration for what's next.

No matter what, I hope this book provides you with some relief and the information you need to tackle your fears and turn a bullying situation into a competitive advantage. I hope that you will no longer get levelled when confronted by female aggression or bullying at work, but are instead strengthened by it and become the action hero in a life that you love.

Part I

Kathryn's Story

This is the story of Kathryn Underwood, a 40-year-old woman who decided to put her hat into the ring for CEO of Kudos Industries. Kudos Industries was an organisation specialising in the development of online betting systems for sports racing and gaming agencies. Kathryn's title was General Manager of Marketing and Strategy, and she had been with Kudos for 12 years. Again, while Kathryn is based on one of Jean-François's and my real clients, all specific details have been changed for the purposes of creating this story. Kudos Industries, for example, is a fictitious company. However, the broad outcomes and learnings from this experience remain the same.

Chapter 1

A chance to change history

Kathryn graduated top of her class in law at a prestigious Ivy League school in the United States. Offers for internship had come in thick and fast, but she turned them all down for a role in the marketing department of a reputable airline with a brand that was sexy and world-class – and a leader who was famous for his gregarious character, fearless nature and penchant for taking creative risks. Her decision paid off, and several years later she was well known in the industry as a product and marketing seer with the gift of foresight and a nose for the next best thing. Joining Kudos was a big career move. The lure of working in what was at the time a start-up organisation in the technology sector enticed her. The thought of having an opportunity to create a new market sector was too good to pass up. She had learned a lot from her previous role with an airline; now it was time to test herself without the crutch of her previous boss.

Kudos Industries' headquarters was in Toronto, the industrial hub of Eastern Canada. Like many fast-growing Toronto-based companies, the culture at Kudos was all about stealth, entrepreneurial genius and world domination. Peter Stringer, its founder, was a charismatic, hard-driving powerhouse full of great ideas with incredible skills of execution, and the additional incentive of having to prove to everyone that he was just as successful as his father, Cornelius Stringer.

Cornelius had made his millions 30 years earlier buying up forests in small towns in northern Ontario, cutting those forests down, and building pulp and paper processing plants to provide Canadians with enough toilet tissue to wipe all their bottoms clean. Investing in a green-fields enterprise and entrusting the building of his fortune to his eldest son meant that he watched the rise of Kudos with obsessive scrutiny. He placed enormous pressure on his son to succeed – along with the threat of disinheritance if anything should go wrong.

So, with an almighty chip on his shoulder and massive shoes to fill, Peter had created a take-no-prisoners culture at Kudos: to win business at all costs, to value results at the expense of relationships. To make it at Kudos, you had to adhere to the FIFO rule – either fit in or f*ck off!

Peter's decision to step back from the CEO role and focus more on innovation and developing other lines of business created an unprecedented opportunity for someone else to take the helm and lead Kudos.

The all-male (except for Kathryn) executive team had been with the organisation since its inception. They had enjoyed the fruits of a business that had a monopoly on the gaming industry; Kudos' online solutions provided the software to most betting engines in North America. They were a market force to be reckoned with. The likelihood of Kathryn successfully winning the role was next to nil given the testosterone-high, incestuous culture of the business, but she decided to go for it anyway.

Kathryn called me in the final days of her preparation to help her take her game to the next level. As her coach and trusted advisor, I got to witness her battle firsthand - all the highs and the lows.

This is her story.

Chapter 2

The battle begins

Kathryn Underwood

I had actually first met Kathryn six years earlier. She was 34 at the time and had just married Bruce, an old flame she had briefly dated back in high school. She and Bruce had rekindled their relationship at their high school reunion in their picturesque hometown of Wakefield, Québec, about 35 kilometres from Canada's capital city of Ottawa.

At our initial meeting, I was struck by Kathryn's talent, leadership potential and striking good looks. Kathryn had piercing sea-blue eyes and long, silky auburn tresses that she kept tied up in a ponytail to keep the focus on her professional persona. She attributed her statuesque, trim and taut figure to her mother, clean eating, and a relentless dedication to yoga five times a week.

Despite her attempts to downplay her physical attributes, Kathryn could not hide her beauty. It was fascinating to watch people meet her for the first time, and men in particular. They'd gawk and fumble, mutter and splutter in her presence. It was hard not to stare at this woman – she was a goddess. Her appearance was only rivalled by her astute intellect, creative mind and down-to-earth personality. She was unaware of how magnificent she was – a triple threat.

When I first met her, Kathryn had the world at her feet, but she kept getting in her own way. She cared too much about what others thought of her. Her need for approval was so high that it made her appear weak and indecisive. She put others first, at the expense of herself and getting results.

In her personal life, a history of failed relationships reflected deeper self-sabotaging tendencies to sacrifice herself and act like a proverbial doormat. It was disconcerting to see how, in the face of finding love, such an extraordinary woman had diminished her light to a dull and wavering flicker.

She wasn't sure when she had decided to compete for the top job at Kudos, but now she had reached the tipping point: there was no turning back. Going public with her decision sealed her fate. She put it all on the line. No more second-guessing herself, and no more beating around the bush.

When I reconnected with Kathryn during her final preparation for interviewing for the CEO role, being a supporting act had become a thing of the past for her. She had undergone a mammoth personal transformation. Heartbreak will do that to you. Her decision to marry Bruce had been a safe option after being trampled on too many times by foreign playboys who had whispered sweet nothings in Mediterranean tongues. They had promised her the world and never delivered. Bruce was a reliable and stoic bookwormish guy who made a good living as a well-known philatelist. (That's the study of stamps and postal history and other related items.)

Methodical and matter of fact, Bruce was the antithesis of her previous gushing flames. His word was his bond. Kathryn traded passion for loyalty and excitement for familiarity. Bruce would never break her heart. The relationship had strengthened her. The princess had toughened up.

As a leader she was now more focused on driving results through others and leading from behind. Some may even have described her as cold. From my perspective, Kathryn had become more of a fighter. She was courageous and strong. Her team was committed and loyal to her. Kathryn had proven that she could get results.

It had been a long time coming and Kathryn was ready to rumble – she was willing to get in the ring and go after what she wanted, and she wanted it bad. But did she have what it took to be the new CEO of Kudos? Would others recognise her as having the 'X' factor? Would she be able to come out on top? Was her superior performance enough to secure her fate?

Preston Steele

Kathryn's competition for the CEO role was Preston Steele. He had more sizzle than a sausage. Some might say his middle name was sleaze. Preston was the kind of guy who slithered around dripping words like maple syrup. He seemed to be able to get away with just about anything. We'd seen him in action from afar, and this man was fierce when he worked a room. Ask just about anyone what they thought about the latest fool he'd double-crossed or any one of the string of women he'd left broken hearted, and the response was usually 'Oh, that's just Preston'.

Preston was not a wimpy yet oh-so-cool metrosexual. He was a ruggedly handsome man with a powerful physique. Well built, in his early 40s, Preston's super-styled salt-and-pepper hair gave him the illusion of wisdom beyond his years. His naturally olive skin and doe-brown eyes contrasted against snow-white teeth to present a picture of perfect health. It was difficult not to notice him – the ultimate snake charmer. Growing up next to a steel mill in the industrial city of Hamilton, Ontario, had given him the motivation to leave behind his impoverished existence with his single mom. He jumped into a new life and never looked back. His mother was lucky if she heard from him at all. He sent the odd Christmas email, but it usually arrived late.

His background in a cutthroat sales environment had equipped him with the skills to play dirty and win. Preston was a political animal. He had mastered the art of networking with all the right people. People either opened the doors for him or kept him out of trouble. From all accounts, he was not particularly smart or driven; however, he was as slick as they come. His greatest gift was the ability to sweet-talk people into doing things for him. Preston was all about minimum effort for high return – and all the glory that went with it. We were impressed that he'd made it this far. He had kicked off his career as a telemarketer to a menagerie of bored and lonely stay-at-home mums in the more affluent areas of Toronto. With licence plates that read 'MOTIV8TED', he was now perfectly matched to his role at Kudos as Vice-President of Business Development.

Despite his popularity, it was hard to imagine people would take a slimy creature like him seriously to steer the Kudos ship. It was widely known that he liked to slather up unsuspecting victims before going in for the kill. But from Kathryn's perspective, she felt she had a real fight on her hands.

Chapter 3

Game on, baby

Day 1: Morning session

Fast-forward a couple of weeks from my and Jean-François's initial meeting with Kathryn and it was showtime! The preparation blitz was a thing of the past. We had worked hard for 12 days, which felt like a flash and a lifetime. We had put together a psychological game plan and win strategy for her climb to the top and get her mentally ready to be match fit when she stepped into the arena against Preston Steele. It had been exhausting for us. Kathryn felt the odds were against her. We had to keep reminding her why she deserved to be there and that she had a chance to help turn the tides for senior women, but we also understood why she was shaky. The rate at which women moved into leadership roles at Kudos was glacial. Worst yet, Kathryn had not gained any momentum and the odds-on heavy favourite 'Mr Golden Boy' Preston Steele had gone up. He was a master schmoozer with all the connections. He won support in a man's world through his sleazy wit, Colgate smile and non-stick coating. Sh*t didn't stick to this guy. If it were a boxing match, he would easily have been the favourite!

Truth be told, Preston didn't consider Kathryn a serious threat. Kathryn heard through the grapevine that he had spread a rumour that she was the token female on the executive team. He spread the word that Kathryn was only there to get them all juiced up with her hot looks and high-heeled shoes. It was clear that Preston considered Kathryn a warm-up fight. He was already planning his next move once he moved into the CEO role and booted her out of the running.

We sat with Kathryn in a large conference room on the 22nd floor at Kudos. Tomorrow she would face the executive hiring committee. It was time for the last dry run. All bets were pretty much up. Kathryn addressed the mock panel, which Jean-François and I formed a part of. She was inspiring, slick and on a roll. She was ready.

Tomorrow the panel would comprise six people from the executive hiring committee: five from the organisation plus an external consultant they'd hired. The external consultant, Emma Darling, was from a reputable executive search firm. Her role was to bring objectivity to the process and help with all the recruitment steps from the ground up.

Jean-François and I knew Emma Darling. She was, without a doubt, a piece of work. We had no idea why she'd been selected to be part of the committee. We thought it was perhaps because she was elegant and flashy and looked the part. The irony was that Emma's attraction to executive recruitment had everything to do with the money, power and glory connected with networking with the who's who in Canadian business. It had nothing to do with helping clients.

Most of us have met people like Emma Darling before – people who put themselves at the centre of the universe. Her skill was building relationships that helped her get a leg up. Once your time was up, she'd forget you faster than a New York minute. For the Emma's of this world, people were dispensable, a means to an end. It was nothing personal.

Knowing that Emma was like this made me nervous. We knew what an opportunist she was. Her modest background made her hungry for a better life. She was the type of woman who would sell her grandmother if she thought it would make her a few bucks. We were curious as to how she'd been representing Kathryn to the hiring committee. She'd probably worked hard to make Kathryn feel like a star. Maybe sold her a line or two and pandered to her insecurities by overwhelming her with praise. She was good at that. Kathryn didn't suspect a thing.

Kathryn and Preston were both candidates from Emma's executive search firm. Everyone knew Emma had a weakness for powerful, rich and good-looking men. We saw her loneliness and believed she'd give up just about everything for love. Hopefully, she hadn't decided to back the person she viewed as the hottest prospect. We'd soon find out.

Kathryn had 90 minutes to present and defend her candidacy. To Kathryn, those 90 minutes felt like forever. She was determined, however. She was going to blow their socks off. Game on, people, it was showtime!

She knew a huge part of her potential success lay in her ability to read her audience. She had to know the committee inside out, warts and all. Information equals power, and the only way she felt she could win this gig was to target their hot spots. She had to know their story - understand what made them tick. Not one to take any chances, she had put two of her best on the case full-time. Tim and Ann were given carte blanche and a fat budget to find out what they could - including digging up any dirt. No holds barred. Kathryn made it clear to her pumped-up team that she'd do whatever it took to win.

What Kathryn's team dug up on Emma left everybody speechless. Tim and Ann had heard that she had a less-than-professional interest in Preston, so they spent a few days waiting in her parking lot to follow her movements and see what she was up to. They staked her out for three days and came up with nothing - and then the unexpected happened. On the fourth day, Tim and Ann followed Emma to a fancy looking apartment in Yorkville. The doorman appeared to know her. It was clear this wasn't her first visit. A few hours later Emma emerged from the building with a man. It was Preston Steele! They watched as Preston pulled Emma closer towards him in a passionate kiss and stroked her lower back.

Emma had been sleeping with the enemy!

Chapter 4

From doormat to warrior

Later on day 1: No more feeling like a loser

The dry run was done. It had gone beautifully. Jean-François and I were back in Kathryn's office, going over a few details and reminiscing about the past. Her training was done. There was no point in going further. In fact, over-preparing was the danger to avoid at this point.

This was Kathryn second attempt to make a play for the head honcho job at Kudos. The first time she tried, she'd cracked under the pressure. Again, what hurt her was her need for approval from other people. During that first attempt she had kept waiting on a sign from the top that she was seen as the right person for the job. As the days passed, the acknowledgement never came, and the self-doubt gnawed away at her confidence until she melted into a puddle of nothing. Trapped in a self-fulfilling prophecy, she withered into a nothing person, forgettable and easy to miss.

I was not exactly sure of when the shift in her psyche happened, and she decided that enough was enough and she was finally ready to play with the big boys and try to beat them at their own game.

I remember her bursting into my office – it must have been four of five years back – with a fiercely determined look in her eyes I'd never seen before. Her look said: 'I've had enough of feeling like a doormat. I'm not taking any more crap from anyone!' She told Jean-François and I that from now on she would be the one with bigger balls, and that she was going to take a swing at anyone who stood in her way. She said to us – and this is a direct quote – 'I've got balls the size of grapefruits! If anybody has a problem with that, I'm not a hard woman to find'.

Back at our wind-down session, I asked her if she could pinpoint a specific event that triggered her change. She wasn't sure and neither were we. Frankly, I don't think she cared about how it happened. She was moving at the speed of light with little regard for consequences and a tunnel-vision focus on the main prize.

As business hours were long over, Kathryn opened a bottle of red wine and poured us all a glass. She needed to unwind. She deserved it. We talked some more and listened to her that night. It occurred to me that she had gone from practising a combat sport just for fun to wanting to go pro and be the best. She used to be someone I would describe as having talent and a few flashy moves, but now she had her practice gloves off and she was ready to get into the ring and give herself the best chance of nailing it.

In truth, Jean-François and I were still not sure if she could pull it off. Her self-esteem was still shaky. Despite all the hot air, we knew her armour was not bulletproof. If she failed, she would need a lot of support. We would be ready either way.

Chapter 5

Backfired booty call

Day 2: 7.30 am

This was the day. The day that would make or break Kathryn's shot at the title. Her interview was at 4.45 pm sharp. Preston Steele's was on immediately after hers.

That morning, Kathryn was in a foul mood. Tim and Ann had just told her about Emma and Preston. Kathryn was in shock but wanted to play it cool and give Emma a chance to do the right thing. She wanted to see just how far Emma would continue playing the game before she revealed to Emma that she knew her secret, so she set up a meeting.

In their meeting, which Kathryn told us about in detail afterwards, Emma paid Kathryn lip service and rolled out the standard platitudes: that the CEO's job was not the be all and end all, how she had every right to be proud of her performance so far, and – wait for it – that whatever happened, she had a great future ahead. It made Kathryn sick to her stomach to hear Emma preparing her for defeat. Knowing Emma was screwing Preston and watching Emma lie to her face was hard to take.

Kathryn had been counting on Emma to be her ally and had buttered her up over the last few weeks, promising her a truckload of business. Now Kathryn realised she had been screwed over by Emma and was furious. She was going to take her down.

'So, Emma, how's Preston's campaign going?' Kathryn asked. 'I'm really relying on you to provide both of us with different ways in which we can present ourselves in the best possible light and secure the position based on who is better equipped for the role. What are your instincts so far? Who do you think is going to make it?'

Kathryn watched as Emma shifted uncomfortably in her seat. 'You are both really neck and neck in this. You're very different. It just depends on what the board is looking for. I'm not sure what else to tell you, Kathryn.' Emma spoke in a quiet voice and dropped her gaze.

'Are you sure you've told me everything Emma? You know our relationship has got to be completely transparent. As my advisor,

I am relying on you to help me make the right decisions', Kathryn told her.

Emma did not answer.

'Nothing to say, Emma?' Kathryn glared at her, refusing to avert her laser-like gaze.

'Nothing more than I shared already, Kathryn', she whispered.

'Well, we both know that's not true', said Kathryn. 'When were you going to tell me that you've been banging Preston?'

Emma went silent.

'Emma! I don't have to tell you what this means for your career. I am going to have to insist that your remove yourself from the selection panel and notify the committee of your conflict of interest. As for me, I haven't decided yet how to make you useful to me. One thing's for sure, I want to know everything you have said about me to Preston. I want to know what you've shared with the panel that could have biased their view of me in your efforts to give Preston the edge.' Kathryn was fuming. 'But for now, just leave. I can't even bear to look at you right now. You make me sick!'

Emma looked grief stricken and scurried away, her face streaming with the crocodile tears of a person who had been found out.

I didn't dare ask Kathryn if she had been expecting some kind of collegial female solidarity. Jean-François and I both knew the answer to that one. Kathryn had a long history of not getting on too well with other women. She had never had such thing as a real and legit girls' club in her professional life. Kathryn's personal belief was that women in power only knew one thing – how to tear each other down. It was a major source of frustration for her in our sessions. She slumped now in her chair and told us that she felt like a fool for thinking it would be any different this time around. We knew Kathryn's tendency to tar all women with the same brush would only exacerbate her feelings of betrayal. In fairness, Kathryn should have been savvier and recognised Emma for who she was. She hadn't read the play and now it had the potential to lead to her undoing.

Even with Emma forced out of the picture, it was hard to know what damage had already been done to her reputation. She needed to find out. The sand in the hourglass was almost out.

Kathryn was incredibly distracted after her run-in with Emma. Jean-François and I needed to get her back on track, and asked her to describe how the meeting with Emma had gone in more detail. She shared snippets of the conversation and told us she'd busted out the heavy artillery. She was not going to lie down quietly. She had dug up enough dirt on Emma to force her to keep a low profile and even the playing field. Emma didn't really have a choice. She had to agree to Kathryn's terms and conditions and was thrown out on her arse.

Time would only tell how much permanent damage Emma's undermining over the last month had done. I cautioned Kathryn and advised her to move through her anger and betrayal as quickly as possible. But she wanted revenge.

When push came to shove, Jean-François and I understood that Emma's behaviour wasn't about Kathryn at all. It wasn't personal. For Emma, it all came down to her gaining favour with the object of her affections in the hope of finding true love. It had backfired on her.

With Emma out of the picture, a new game plan was needed. Kathryn had to come up with a new strategy to win the race – and fast.

Chapter 6

When reality bites

Day 2: 8.30 am

We needed to take some time out from all the political lobbying and refocus. When all was said and done, one simple truth remained: Kathryn was the better candidate for the CEO role. There was no question. We knew it, we'd done our psychological evaluation and put her through her paces, and we could prove it.

Here's what put Kathryn ahead:

- *Business sense:* Kathryn had a broader understanding of Kudos's business than Preston. Preston had street-smarts credibility, but he was clueless about almost everything else. He was strictly an operations guy, focused on ensuring his people get stuff done so he could look good. Kathryn was more well-rounded, a blue-sky thinker with loads of substance.
- *Vision:* Kathryn had a daring and innovative vision for Kudos. She knew that introducing new technologies would transform the way Kudos did business and reinvigorate their main revenue streams. She was also prepared for implementing these new technologies. Creativity ran through her veins. She could take this business to a whole new level.
- *Leadership:* Kathryn was an outstanding leader. She was humble and lead by example. Her track record spoke for itself. Building powerful and effective teams was second nature to her – period.
- *Enthusiasm:* Kathryn was dedicated and hungry – more so than anyone else on the executive team. Her desire for progress and to catapult the company into another stratosphere was unparalleled. This was what she did. This was who she was.
- *Track record:* Kathryn knew how to streamline costs and turn Kudos into a well-oiled machine. She'd done it before with all her departments. She could do it again. These were the facts, and she had the numbers to prove it.

Kathryn had the goods. She was focused, clear in where she wanted to take Kudos, and had the data to back up every claim she made. She had depth. Putting her into the top job made sense.

So, how on earth did Preston even get in the running?

Preston had the edge on two counts. Firstly, he looked the part. From all accounts he was an average leader, with nothing remarkable about him. But, damn, he was slick! He said all the right things and people loved him. He was a pimped-out con who had everybody fooled.

Preston was also a master networker and friends with all the who's who. Rumour had it he had the skinny on many of his powerful friends, and that made him dangerous and untouchable.

As lunchtime approached, we remained silent for a while. It was clear that Kathryn was not aiming for a moral victory. No prizes would be awarded for coming in second, and Kathryn was not going to take solace from impressing the committee in a losing effort. She was the best candidate, and she wanted to win. She was convinced she could pull it off.

We wanted to believe it too!

Chapter 7

Riding the swell to catch the wave

Day 2: Noon

Kathryn was in a room nearby having a quick bite with her husband, Bruce. Jean-François and I could hear her through the paper-thin walls – she was not feeling good. Bruce tried to calm her down, but it didn't work. His support was shut down and he ended up saying all the wrong things. It was hard to listen to, and we felt sorry for him.

It didn't help that on the emotional intelligence scale Bruce was a zero. He just didn't seem to get her. I'm not sure he ever had. He had no idea how much his wife had changed. Kathryn wouldn't allow herself to be second best anymore. Her fighting spirit had raised her from sleepwalking through life to striving for more. She was a fighter now. No more apologies. No more asking for permission. She had reprogrammed herself for success. Kathryn was ready to take on Preston Steele.

Bruce's attempts to soothe his wife were cringe-worthy.

'Everything's going to be great, babe', he told her. 'You've got nothing to lose. You've got a good job and a great life with me, anything else is just cream. In the grand scheme of things, you've already won! Just give it your best shot!' Jean-François and I both winced. We could imagine Kathryn bristling as she stayed silent.

We were surprised Kathryn didn't knock Bruce out after that. She loved her husband, but knew he wasn't made for tackling the tough stuff. We're pretty sure Kathryn had already mentally checked out and was preserving her energy for the real showdown. She was anxious to finish her lunch and get back into the ring.

A few minutes later, we saw them in the hallway. Bruce wished her good luck and told her that he loved her. She mumbled something back. She was far away – no longer interested in being the loving wife and mother. She was focused on one thing and one thing only: beating Preston Steele.

Chapter 8

Dazed and confused

Day 2: Early afternoon

While we waited in a small meeting room, Kathryn's two main advisors burst in with an update and all hell broke loose. The word on the street was that Emma Darling was back at it. She'd been spreading rumours that Kathryn was not a good enough people-leader for the CEO gig. Emma said that Kathryn wasn't someone who could galvanise the troops beyond her inner circle. She said Kathryn alienated people.

The extent of Emma's treachery finally hit home. Preston was not the bad guy after all, not in the grand scheme of things. Preston was not even Kathryn's biggest adversary. That role was filled by Emma Darling, conspiring and plotting Kathryn's demise just to please her boyfriend. At the end of the day, this was all about sex.

In that moment, reality hit.

Kathryn realised she would probably not get the job. And it wasn't because of a sleazy salesman like Preston, or a male-dominated company culture or even because she was a woman. She had been sucker punched. She'd been up against a sister with her own personal agenda who had actively plotted to knock her out of the running for a different kind of prize.

Then someone who claimed to have seen the results of Kathryn's psychological testing leaked out a story that gave legs to Emma's fabrications about her. Along similar lines, Preston was held to be the better candidate because he tested well as an inspiring leader. This was absolute garbage, but the gossip was out of control, and it weakened Kathryn's positioning.

You've got to hand it to Emma. Her ability to spread rumours about Kathryn was like an untreated cancer that had taken over Kudos.

I know that the power of falsehoods and twisted truths cannot be underestimated. In all my years as an executive coach, I've witnessed countless takedowns and been privy to the fast destruction of promising candidates based on lies and gossip. With Kathryn, Jean-François and I knew that we could not waste a moment. It was time to get into a huddle and tweak the final game plan. Even if Kathryn didn't stand a strong chance, she would not go down without a fight. We came up with five strategies to handle all eventualities:

- *Strategy 1: Don't be defensive.* The first strategy was to remind Kathryn that she should not under any circumstances appear defensive during her presentation. She had to be the duck gliding on the pond while paddling furiously underneath the surface. Cool, poised and collected. Bitterness never wins any points.
- *Strategy 2: Talk about the elephant in the room.* We advised Kathryn to raise the leadership reputation gossip right from the get-go. There was no sense in waiting. We already knew what everyone had heard. She needed to flag it and address it. Better to nip the sucker in the bud and clear their attention to focus on the good stuff.
- *Strategy 3: Don't out the relationship between Emma and Preston.* Women who lash out publicly at other women end up getting punished for it. Better to force Emma to withdraw from the process and fess up to what she had done herself rather than talk about it. We were all in agreement. If we played it like this, we had a shot at being able to turn the rumours to our advantage. We needed a good angle, though.
- *Strategy 4: Don't play the woman card.* We advised Kathryn to argue that Kudos Industries had never seen leadership like hers before but not mention gender. Kudos needed a sea of change to reinvigorate the business. Her plan? To work with the business to create think tanks to gather up the best ideas from the floor and act on them. Kathryn was going to share her ideas on how she would empower people at all levels to unleash their creativity and enhance business performance.
- *Strategy 5: Inspire the committee with her vision of what the organisation would look like with her leading it.* Kathryn's goal was to transform Kudos's unhealthy corporate culture so it could become a

constructive and great place to work. Her closing statement had us all inspired. Her new vision of the Kudos world meant that all employees had agency as leaders and were encouraged to take personal responsibility for creating the new culture at Kudos as a great place to work. 'It's what the company needs', she was going to say. 'The time for change is now, and I am the person to make it happen.'

The mood in the meeting room was intense at this point. We were all staring at Kathryn. Jean-François and I knew she was the best candidate for the role, but we were concerned that her brilliant pitch would not strike the right chord for all the committee members.

Someone – perhaps Ann, another of Kathryn's main advisors – had a great idea. She proposed that Kathryn do the unexpected and demonstrate 'live' how her team leadership cultivated high performance by inviting her direct reports into the presentation to give their views on her as a leader. The committee could then decide for themselves. We were all sold on the idea.

Let's face it, with the stakes so high we had everything to gain and nothing to lose.

Chapter 9

The lowdown

Day 2: 3.15 pm

After Kathryn's inspiring run-though, the mood then flipped from psyched up to sombre. Bob, Kathryn's sad sack of a sponsor, showed up and informed us, from all indications, things didn't look good. He told us it was unlikely that the majority would vote for Kathryn. Talk about raining on her parade! Now was not the time to threaten Kathryn's positive psyche. Bob's comments felt like a deliberate attempt to throw her off her game. She already knew where things were at and didn't need to be thrown any more lethal truth bombs.

Jean-François and I pulled him to one side and gave him the hard word.

'Look, Bob, we appreciate your insights, but what would really help Kathryn right now is some information on who's in that room. Tell Kathryn everything she needs to know to have greater impact. Help her or leave.' We pointed at the doorway.

'Well', he said, taking a deep breath, 'there's Mr Rosenberg. He's the oldest guy on the committee. He retired from corporate life a few years back but keeps hanging around to give his life some semblance of a purpose between golf games. He's been with Kudos forever. But don't waste your time with him, he's a lost cause. Plus, he and Preston are tight. At best, he'll be pleasantly surprised by Kathryn's presentation because Preston and Emma have set a low bar on Kathryn'. He turned to Kathryn. 'He's the kind of old fart to tell you as much.'

So, could Kathryn do enough to change his vote? No way.

1-0 Preston.

Bob continued, sneering. 'Then there's Susan White. She's an old-school Kudos veteran. She scratched and clawed her way to the top and was the first woman to make it onto the executive team – as a VP Human Resources, but still. I know she's got a good relationship with Preston too. She's also got a reputation for blocking other women climbing too far up the ladder. I think it's because she gets off on being in power way too much to share the spotlight. I tried to get a sense from her as to whether she was pro Kathryn or not, but she froze me out.'

What we found out later was that Kathryn was being informally mentored by Susan White. Susan had reluctantly agreed to work with Kathryn to try to shift her reputation as an aggressive she-male with no heart. But Susan didn't really want Kathryn to get the job. She felt it would threaten her position on the executive team, and she didn't want to compete with her. Instead, her approach was to put Kathryn down, and criticise and blame her. Years later, Kathryn admitted to feeling beaten up every time she had a catch-up with Susan. We found out that Susan hadn't defended the rumours about Kathryn either, even though she knew they weren't true. She claimed she didn't want to get involved.

2-0 Preston.

Bob kept on with the run-down. Our hopes still rested on the three remaining committee members – Mr Faris, Mr Levine and Ms Huffington.

Over the past few weeks, Jean-François and I had helped Kathryn tailor specific parts of her presentation to appeal to all the committee members in some way. Perhaps we could still find a glimmer of hope – or so we thought, until party-killer Bob passed on that Mr Levine was on the fence and Ms Huffington was now on the Preston bandwagon. That slimy bastard had canoodled his way in yet again. Maybe he was sleeping with her too? We wouldn't put it past him!

Truth be told, Mr Faris was the only one who was in Kathryn's corner. He was an old friend of the Stringers and a very clever man. He had seen right through Preston's bluster and knew that new blood was what Kudos needed to reinvent itself. Besides, he and Kathryn did have a history of sorts. He had originally hired her way back in the day. He had been a fan ever since – quietly and in the background, but a fan, nonetheless.

Bob sighed heavily again, his whole demeanour sweating defeat. We had to get him out of there before Kathryn got a whiff of his surrender. If he did, we were ready to lynch him, but he didn't get the chance. Kathryn cut him off and put us all out of our misery.

'Enough!' she said. 'I have heard enough. Bob's predictions may be based on good intel but it's beside the point. If I thought like that, I wouldn't have moved up from middle management. When you think like a loser, you become one! I'm done with all this loser talk. Bob, get out!' She pointed at the door, and he slithered out.

I really admired Kathryn at this point. Her transformation from doormat to warrior had been impressive. She refused to believe that changing the minds of old man Rosenberg and the rest of them was impossible. She was not about to find reasons to quit.

The reality was that deep down Kathryn knew she was the better candidate. She just had to try to find a way to convince the committee she was the only choice, notwithstanding Emma's poisoning of the well.

'If they can't see it, it's up to me to open their eyes', she said with determination. 'If they're scared, it's up to me to reassure them. If they are not ready for me, I'll find a way to show I am the only choice. It's my time to shine!' Kathryn was smiling and eager to get in the room. One way or another, a decision had to be made, and she was tired of waiting.

Tim proposed that Kathryn show up to the presentation with, and I quote, 'a big-arse leather whip to beat the committee into submission'. Everyone laughed. The mood in the room had lifted. We were ready to win. We had no room for negative naysayers at this stage of the game.

Chapter 10

The showdown

Day 2: 4.35 pm

Kathryn had dressed herself for power and impact that day. Her new designer red crepe suit contrasted beautifully against her silk cream shirt. Her long auburn hair fell naturally down her back, which gave her a much more relaxed and quietly confident demeanour than the usual tightly pulled-back French braid. Lustrous, creamy pearl earrings completed her look of elegant confidence.

The presentation was about to start. With 10 minutes to go, Jean-François and I went through any last-minute details with Kathryn. She was calm – she knew her stuff and she looked the part. Tim went over all the key points one last time. He'd arranged for her entire team to show up in the last 20 minutes of the presentation so they could talk about Kathryn's leadership skills and hammer home how awesome she was.

We looked over and saw Ann in the corner of the room discreetly working on a concession speech. She winked at us. It was her job to prepare for every eventuality and we had a few scenarios left to consider. We weren't sure what tack Kathryn would end up taking if she lost this race, but we figured she had about three potential options. One: she could right-out quit the company. And let's face it, no-one would blame her given the dog and pony show she was being asked to put up with. Two: she could bow out gracefully and take some time off. Three: she could leverage the committee's guilt into her preferred position. Kathryn didn't let on what she had decided to do.

There was a knock at the door. Somebody showed up to announce the committee was ready and Kathryn had to leave right away. At this point, we still thought we had a shot, but it was a long shot. We had no doubt in our minds that Kathryn would make a remarkable CEO, and she was ready for it. We also knew that to have a female CEO in a male-dominated environment would buck existing trends and reinvigorate the organisation. Kathryn was fighting against institutional barriers and entrenched social norms – it would be a miracle if she could tear down those walls and start to turn the tides at Kudos.

If she lost, we bet our money on her quitting straightaway. Too much was on the line now. She couldn't stay on and play second fiddle to Preston Steele. Not in this lifetime. Kathryn put on her jacket and marched toward the door. She was ready and in the zone. All bets were off now.

She walked into the meeting room and stood at the head of the boardroom table and began: 'Good afternoon, everyone. Thank you for the opportunity to be considered as the CEO of Kudos. I am deeply honoured. I hope that in the next hour, I will be able to convince you why I am the right choice to lead Kudos into the future.'

Chapter 11

Pulling the rabbit out of a hat

Day 2: 6.30 pm

Kathryn's presentation was a thing of beauty. Everything went perfectly and according to plan, and the presentation was stunning, pure poetry in motion. Kathryn was on. The core of her speech, where she shared her vision for the company, blew everyone away. She had everyone transfixed. She delivered her punchlines flawlessly. Hell, Jean-François and I felt like running out of the room to go buy shares in the company!

The inspired energy that permeated the room when Kathryn's team walked in sealed the deal. And, for 20 minutes or so, we heard very open and genuine experiences of what it was like to work with her. It made me emotional!

Kathryn's team shared a great mix of storytelling, anecdotes, a few well-delivered self-deprecating jokes and some heartfelt moments. Together, they issued a raw and authentic plea for more from a bunch of talented people thriving under Kathryn's leadership. She presented well, and was poised for greatness and ready for success. Kathryn was engaging and inspiring as an empowering people leader – a visionary who set a clear direction while leveraging her team's strengths to the max.

Kathryn then surprised us all by pulling a final white rabbit out of the hat. Towards the end of her presentation, she went completely off script and talked about the deficit of women in leadership positions at Kudos. She spoke passionately about the glass ceiling that remained pervasive, and how hard it was to try to succeed in that world. She told the hiring committee how she had always had to work harder than her male colleagues to get noticed, and how stressful it was to always have to be better, stronger and faster to get ahead.

'I don't want my gender to be an issue in your decision', Kathryn told them. 'I want to be awarded the job for being myself, for being seen by you as having the greatest potential. Because you see me as the best leader for Kudos' future.'

A long pause followed. Kathryn stopped speaking for what felt like a very long time. We all started to get a little nervous, not knowing what was coming next. She didn't have much time left. Was that a wrap? And then she did it. She had left the best until last. One by one she walked over to each member of the committee, looked them straight in the eye and spoke to them directly.

This part of her closing argument put her at great personal risk, but she went for it anyway. The first person she addressed was Mrs White.

'Mrs White, you have the reputation of not helping other women out. We have both had our differences in the past. But it's time for change. Let another woman sit at the table beside you. I'd like that woman to be me', she said sincerely.

Next up was Mr Rosenberg.

'Mr Rosenberg, how would you feel about being led by a woman? Be honest', she insisted. 'What about by a strong and confident woman with bold views that differ from yours? How would that be for you Mr Rosenberg?'

Jean-François and I didn't know how far she was going to get with this line of questioning, but we admired her for her bravery. And then she delivered the home run.

'At the end of the day, me becoming CEO should not be about fears of female domination and power struggles. I know how to bring people together. I know how to get them to focus on Kudos's mission and value proposition, and how to drive us to greater heights.'

Everyone in the room was blown away by her candour and conviction. Old Rosenberg was shaking like a leaf. I figured he had soiled his pants thinking she had made it and won everybody over. Kathryn had given an unbelievable performance. She had taken a big risk presenting with such frankness, but it could still go either way.

Chapter 12

The con artist

Day 2: 7.30 pm

Preston had been stealthily planning his attack for weeks. Emma had, of course, been incredibly useful to him. She'd given him the lowdown on Kathryn's vulnerabilities and he was ready to stick the knife in. He had learnt to leverage the power of pillow talk to give him the edge in his career.

After all, it was Peter Stringer's wife, Delilah, who had really paved the way for him at Kudos. He'd met her one Friday afternoon having drinks at Ki, a funky modern Japanese bar and eatery in Toronto's financial district. He had no idea who she was at first and had just taken her for one of the regular bar stars that hung out at high-end establishments after work to try to pick up rich, eligible men. She played right into his hands. He thought of her as like many wives of the powerful men he knew: over-processed, lonely as hell and hiding a messy drinking problem.

The affair lasted as long as it took him to get the job at Kudos – all of five minutes. Delilah had convinced her husband that Kudos needed a business development gun like Preston to help them increase market share. His network of A-list connections made him a very attractive proposition for Peter, who wasn't much into socialising and was happy to pass this on to Preston to make sure they were talking to all the right people.

Delilah supported Preston's decision to make a play for her husband's job. It was her way of appeasing him so he wouldn't blow the lid on her infidelity. Part of the deal was that she would give him insider information on her family's plans to build the intangible value of Kudos to position it for an eventual sale. She shared with him the buttons to push to get the other members of the executive on his side, telling him how to engage every board member and what to say to impress her husband, Peter, and his father, Cornelius.

Preston's presentation hit the mark. It didn't matter that he didn't have a proven track record of success or that he'd been with the company for less than a year. He played right into their hands, and they loved what they heard. Many of the board members commented later about how incredible it was how he'd nailed their vision for the future. Preston was seen as a genius.

Chapter 13

The final countdown

Day 2: 8.15 pm

Back in the 'green room' with Kathryn, the mood was manic. We all believed that Kathryn still had a shot for the CEO title. At this point, Jean-François and I had no idea what Preston had been up to or Delilah's involvement in all this. Had we known, we would have advised her very differently.

Amid all the high-fiving and gushing over Kathryn, people were trying to get the inside scoop on how she'd done. We were wondering whether the committee would deliberate all night or take their time and prolong the suspense. Maybe they'd call the candidates back for a second round of questioning. It was hard to say.

Then a bomb went off. We got wind that Preston had gone way over time in his presentation – which was technically not allowed. We also heard that he'd talked at length about Kathryn. We heard from someone inside who claimed to have seen an early version of Preston's speech and swore to us it was very complimentary of Kathryn. We thought that this was all part of his master game plan. Show someone close to Kathryn a positive version of everything he would say about her, and then turn on her behind closed doors.

Preston's strategy paid off. The news came in. Preston Steele had been anointed the new CEO of Kudos. It had been a fait accompli. We all felt heavy and deflated, as if the air had been sucked out of the room.

At this stage, we still didn't know how much Emma's manipulation had played a role in Kathryn's defeat. But we weren't naive enough to think that anyone couldn't have been negatively skewed by the filth she had spewed about Kathryn. We knew that Mrs White had also remained a passive resistor. She had the opportunity to defend Kathryn's reputation but didn't. As far as we were concerned, she was as culpable as Emma for orchestrating Kathryn's inevitable defeat.

Chapter 14

She's left the building

Six weeks later

It had been six weeks since Kathryn lost out to Preston, and she was nowhere to be found. Nobody had seen her. Inside sources told me and Jean-François she had hopped on a plane that same night and flew by herself to an undisclosed location, somewhere far away in the sun. Rumour had it she had drunk herself into oblivion and passed out somewhere under a palm tree.

While we weren't sure about the rumours, we did know Kathryn had sent in her resignation first thing the next morning. Preston did not accept it at first, convinced she would come to her senses and come back. Her departure had him spooked. He had counted on her to still be at Kudos. He had crafted a huge 'I need you – I can't do this without you' speech, which was in fact true. He had planned to delegate most of the job to her while he took all the credit for the company's success. But Kathryn didn't bite.

He next offered her everything to convince her to stay – more status, money, perks, the whole nine yards – but her decision remained unyielding.

Her reply was short and to the point. 'You've got to be kidding, Preston', she scoffed. 'With everything that I know about you, I hope you choke on it!'

Her supporters were still chuckling about her response weeks after she left.

The Kudos board had underestimated her too. They knew what they had in her, but never thought that she would walk. They figured she'd be like other women they'd worked with, grateful for still having a well-paid position and understanding of the fact that she's lost out to a candidate better suited to the CEO position than her.

It didn't take long for them to realise that in Preston they had a good-looking sack of nothing. He didn't have the goods to be the new CEO of Kudos. But it was too late; Kathryn had vanished, and Kudos began to internally combust. Without Kathryn's vision, ability to manage innovation and skills in execution, Kudos was left vulnerable to external forces and the outdated thinking of its founders.

Chapter 15

The crash landing

Months later

Over the following months, Kathryn kept us all guessing. Jean-François and I didn't know where she'd gone, and we were worried about her. To go from flying so close to the sun to a monumental crash landing had to have been devastating, even for a resilient woman like Kathryn.

Kathryn cleverly managed perceptions of her departure with great cunning. Her decision to leave had left Kudos's godfathers shell-shocked. They wiped her off as foolish, believing that her female emotions had gotten in the way of her making the right and rational decision. Secretly, they respected her more than ever.

The truth was that Kathryn had hit rock bottom. The stress of all the lies, the undermining antics, white-anting, gaslighting, bullying and the Stringer family drama had finally taken its toll – and Kathryn was emotionally spent.

In her heart of hearts, her idealistic self had always believed that, in the end, the best person for the job would succeed and justice would prevail. To accept that she had been upstaged by an imposter like Preston was more than she could bear. It really was a man's world – a world she now believed was always going to be an unfair playing field.

Kathryn spent close to one year hiding out from her corporate life at her lake house in Muskoka. It was an idyllic spot, featuring a quaint log cottage surrounded by bursts of brightly coloured red and purple rhododendrons and a green mirrored lake. This had always been her sanctuary, the one place she could find peace. Not even poor old Bruce could break through the 10-foot wall she had built around herself.

What plagued Kathryn the most were the lengths to which Emma had gone to sabotage her career. And she did it all for the occasional romp with a dickhead like Preston. She couldn't understand how anyone could be so cruel and vindictive. Then there was her mentor, Mrs White. She'd had every opportunity to save Kathryn's reputation and hadn't even tried. Kathryn felt she had been damned from every angle.

She started to wonder whether it was always the loud talkers with no substance who made it to the top in the end. Even so, the fact that she hadn't made it was a reality she couldn't accept.

An overwhelming feeling of disillusionment and betrayal sent her spiralling down a tunnel of darkness, and the black dog barked so loudly that it blinded her to any glimmers of hope. She had always thought of herself as strong and together. Yet here she was, feeling kicked to the curb with no energy left to fight back. Not even a whisper.

Months later, Kathryn called Jean-François and asked him to come and see her. He could hear it in her voice. She was displaying all the signs of someone who was suffering from the hidden epidemic we had encountered so many times before – that of someone who had been repeatedly pushed around at work. The cumulative impact of Emma undermining her abilities and assassinating her character, coupled with Mrs White's blatant lack of support and underlying bullying, plus years of being blocked from career opportunities, had taken its toll. This once-powerful woman who didn't take crap from anyone had lost herself.

Kathryn was like many who suffer the toll of emotional abuse at work; at first, and even as it magnified, she didn't really acknowledge it was happening. She had found several reasons to rationalise the mistreatment, aggression and bullying. She passed it off as bad behaviour or as someone having a crappy day.

Jean-François and I understood the extent of the damage. We also knew that for women bullied by other women, the psychological trauma tends to be felt a lot more deeply. Kathryn had experienced the mistreatment from all sides. From men she almost expected it. But from other women? She had expected better from them. Weren't they supposed to help her? Women were already so under-represented in leadership roles – surely it was up to women in positions of power to 'part the Red Sea' as much as possible, to help increase female representation at the top?

Jean-François helped Kathryn come to terms with what had happened to her. Naming the pain was the first step, and liberation came with that acknowledgement. She became aware of how her self-esteem had been eroding with every new attack, until she had folded.

As the days passed, Kathryn worked through her shock and anger to accept the reality of what she'd gone through. She realised the challenge she faced wasn't just about having to navigate her way through a man's world of work; it was also about coming to terms with the fact that if she wanted to get back into the ring, she needed to be more astute about her adversaries and her supporters, male and female. She needed to be better prepared than she had been. Her naivety had clouded her judgement.

The desire to fight back strengthened Kathryn's resolve to make a comeback. And then one day in spring, almost two years later, Kathryn dusted the dirt from her wings and prepared to have another crack at the sun.

Chapter 16

Karma's a bitch

A new era

Kudos had once ruled the gaming industry. Now it was barely recognisable as a tech power player. With a muppet at the helm, Peter
Stringer begged his father, Cornelius, to step in and try to save the
family's legacy from complete ruination.

Jean-François and I heard from Kathryn that both Peter and
Cornelius had tried to contact her and left messages on her phone
begging her to return. She would never go back.

Shortly after she lost out to Preston, Kathryn received word from
the owner of Joker Inc. Joker had always played second fiddle to
Kudos. When they heard that Kudos had let the brains behind their
transformation go, and that she was back in town, they wooed her
relentlessly.

And then, exactly one year, 11 months and 20 days after she
walked out of Kudos, Kathryn became the new COO of Joker.

As for Kudos, the market showed its lack of faith in CEO Preston
Steele, and their share value plummeted. Kudos became a vulnerable
enterprise that was ripe for takeover, and Joker now dominated the
gaming industry with their latest product developments and pioneering mindset. Behind closed doors, something else was brewing. The
board of Kudos manoeuvred to merge with Joker and save what was
left of the company. Even the Stringers were kept out of the deal.
Their inability to keep their own personal issues out of the business
had cost Kudos way too much and the board still hadn't figured out
what to do with them. In the meantime, the deal was completed
with Joker holding 50.1 per cent of the shares of Kudos. Things were
finally about to change.

It was late September when Kudos called a press conference with
all its stakeholders and the media. Jean-François and I were invited
to attend. Kudos's chairman, Walter Strozzaprezzi, looked nervous
as he made his way up to the podium. Kudos had received a load
of bad press about its plummeting share price, and we were expecting
bad news.

Looking very GQ, Walter stood up in his navy pinstriped suit and monogrammed cufflinks, and made his announcement in a thick Italian accent. 'Welcome everyone. Thank you for coming today. I am sure you are all wondering why we have called you here'. He looked quite agitated.

We were all getting ready to get the tissues out, thinking the worst. We thought it was strange that there wasn't a Stringer in sight!

'Today marks a momentous day in Kudos history. As you know, we haven't been doing too well lately. But we've decided to turn things around. We've had our butts kicked by Joker Inc. for long enough. We've decided if you can't beat 'em, join 'em. We will be joining forces with Joker.'

Jean-François and I were stunned by his announcement. The room went silent. After the initial shock, we couldn't help but feel relieved that Kudos wasn't going down the gurgler.

Walter could see by the stunned looks on everyone's faces that we were all taken aback by the news.

'I can see many of you were not expecting this. But we are really excited about Kudos becoming part of the Joker family. And, on a more personal note, we are thrilled to make another important announcement.'

Yet another announcement? You could have heard a pin drop.

'Ladies and gentlemen, it took a lot of persuading; however, we are thrilled to announce the new CEO of Joker Inc. – please welcome Kathryn Underwood!'

A breathtaking flame-haired Kathryn stepped up on the stage, her piercing blue eyes beaming with pride.

Walter continued to honour her. 'Kathryn is the reason Joker has single-handedly taken over the market with its latest product innovations. Ladies and gentlemen, put your hands together for Kathryn Underwood!'

Kathryn walked over to the podium. 'Thanks, Walter. Thanks, everyone. I am sure for many of you this has come as a huge shock. I must admit I even surprised myself when I decided to take on this role. But the offer was too good to pass up, and I am ready. I learned a lot about myself in the last few years, about the kind of leader I want to be, about how I want to be remembered. They say that we learn the most from failure. Well, my failures have made me better, wiser and stronger. I am reinvigorated by the challenge to lead the new Joker into a limitless future. Thank you!'

The audience stood, applauded and cheered.

Karma can be a real bitch!

Part II

The sisterhood paradox at play

I hope you are feeling energised by Kathryn's tale from part I and inspired by an extraordinary woman who was able to turn a disastrous situation into stuff that legends are made of. Watching her handle the ups and downs of a tumultuous ride gave me butterflies in my stomach - until they started to fly in formation.

In part II, I provide a more profound investigation into the psychology of what, why and how of female aggression at work. You will be able to spot who's who in your workplace zoo. You'll bone up on the tools and techniques you need to be able to take the control back and lead these situations to your advantage. You'll learn how channel your inner warrior and step into the eye of the storm with confidence and courage - and even become strengthened by it.

Because changing the world will take all of us. Your voice and your deeds matter.

Are you ready?

Chapter 17

Men rule the world, still

America has forged this success while utilizing, in large part, only half of the country's talent. For most of our history, women – whatever their abilities – have been relegated to the sidelines. Only in recent years have we begun to correct that problem.

Warren Buffett

Kathryn's experiences at Kudos reflect a stark reality. As much as we would like to believe women have made progress in the workforce, we have not. The vigorous debates continued by Sheryl Sandberg (with her book *Lean In: Women, Work, and the Will to Lead*) and many others like her highlight the fact that gender-related bias still exists, and we are no closer to getting ahead to any meaningful change.

So, as much as we wish things were different – and some would like to believe that the problem has been corrected – men still rule the world.

The fossilised rate of progress

To illustrate, data from 2020–21 shows that in Australian businesses, men make up roughly 80 per cent of all CEOs, and hold 67.5 per cent of key management, 67 per cent of board positions and 82 per cent of all board chairs.[30] Women in power are a minority in senior leadership positions. The stunted movement of women into senior leadership roles means, overall, women are going backwards not forwards, particularly in Australia. In other parts of the world, the perspective isn't more uplifting – although the Nordic countries are leading the race in female representation and empowerment, with Sweden, Iceland and Norway at the top.[31]

The perennial glass ceiling remains a steadfast institutional barrier. (These days I think the glass has turned into concrete! We're just not breaking through enough.) Gender discrimination, unappealing stereotypes and the lack of support for motherhood also mean that women are less likely to make a play for higher-profile roles, seeing defeat as imminent.

The under-representation of women at the upper echelons of business is not a new story, yet it is even harder to believe when we know that organisations that hire women into senior positions perform way better financially. In fact, Australia's Workplace Gender Equality Agency (WGEA) reported that increasing the number of women in leadership positions can create an improved market value of between $52 million and $70 million for the average Australian organisation.[32]

The stunted movement of women into senior leadership roles means, overall, women are going backwards not forwards, particularly in Australia.

In conversation with Dr Sandy Chong, former President of the United Nations Association of Australia (WA) and Expert Network Member of the World Economic Forum (WEF), she shared research showing that 'when you have 30 per cent of women on boards, you have a 55 per cent increase in sales, 63 per cent increase in return equity and a 56 per cent increase in vested capital'.

Quite simply, placing women into strategic roles equals economic prosperity, end of story. So, what's the problem?

Let's start with how women like Kathryn are being rewarded for their contributions. In terms of salary, men and women still differ substantially in terms of pay, with the United Nations estimating the world salary gap between the sexes still sits at around 20 per cent.[33] In Australia, this gap is 12 per cent, based on full-time average weekly earnings – meaning women would need to work an additional 44 days a year to earn the same as men.[34]

As for promotions, women receive them less frequently than men and are even less likely to move into more senior roles. Case in point: Jean-François and I know that Kathryn would have earned at least 20 per cent less than Preston on becoming the CEO of Kudos.

Damned if you do, damned if you don't

For Kathryn, it was both the glass and sisterhood ceilings at Kudos that blocked her rise in the organisation. Equally, other barriers such as the very male-oriented organisational culture, and a lack of access to high-quality and interested mentors and sponsors, hurt her ability to acquire the level of organisational support she needed to secure a position at the executive table.

But another factor was also at play. Jean-François and I believe that Kathryn's personality transformation from doormat to 'badass' did not help her cause either. From a psychological perspective, we know that neither ends of the spectrum tend to create a favourable impression of a female leader wanting to enhance her career.

Researchers call this phenomenon the 'double-bind effect'. Also known as 'stereotype threat', it is defined as a social and economic reprisal for behaving counter-stereotypically. It's why America Ferrera's monologue in *Barbie* rang so true and got everyone talking. Here's a snippet to remind you:

> It is literally impossible to be a woman ... You have to be a boss, but you can't be mean ... You have to be a career woman, but also always be looking out for other people. You have to answer for men's bad behaviour, which is insane, but if you point that out, you're accused of complaining ... You have to never get old, never be rude, never show off, never be selfish, never fall down, never fail, never show fear, never get out of line. It's too hard!

This lends itself to asking the question – can the psychology of the double-bind effect be counteracted, or is it so interwoven within our societal fabric that it cannot be unpicked?

Being aware of this double bind and learning how to proactively manage it is a great place to start unravelling these metaphorical knots. As an example, acting like a guy at work does women a disservice as does the perception of being overly emotional and acquiescent.

Without a doubt, this is a tricky catch-22 situation that is difficult to navigate. Because women don't typically have the same access to higher-level leadership opportunities, they often feel compelled to engage in behaviours that are perceived as 'unwomanly'. However, if they vocalise their accomplishments – such as daring to ask for a salary increase – they are often dubbed overly ambitious and perceived as aggressive when simply being assertive. Research illustrates how both men and women view other women negatively when they ask for what they want.

It appears that women are damned if they do and damned if they don't!

This sparked an interesting discussion that bubbled up at the research roundtable I ran with 10 reputable and trail-blazing senior women recently. I asked the women whether we should really expect every woman who's 'made it' to help other women just because they are of the same gender. And does the impact of a woman being aggressive or 'unkind' hurt so much more because we don't expect to be treated poorly by other women? Is a reset of our expectations of professional women required?

Here's the commentary from participant Karen Bradshaw, a well-respected senior female lawyer and Chief People Officer from the resources sector:

> *You can't expect every woman to be an incredible coach, advocate or mentor. We don't expect this of every man, so it is unfair to require it of every woman. So, if they can't do that, that's fine, but don't be doing the other stuff, pushing people down.*

Whatever your thoughts on this, I'd like to reframe it this way. Imagine if women in positions of power all committed to lifting other women at work. Might that be the change we need to see if we are to shift the power in a game we are losing right now?

Food for thought.

But let's go back to Kathryn for a moment.

Her sudden evolution into an assertive, gun-toting cowgirl with moral fortitude eroded her reputation as an easy-going high achiever and weakened her candidacy for the CEO role at Kudos. Go figure!

Imagine if women in positions of power all committed to lifting other women at work. Might that be the change we need to see if we are to shift the power in a game we are losing right now?

But it doesn't stop there. Strong evidence suggests that women viewed as powerful are often also perceived as intimidating, abnormal and unattractive. In an article in *The New York Times*, Adam Bryant shared interviews with four executives on succeeding in business as women. A strong message came through that many women won't ask for what they want, for fear of their strong leadership becoming synonymous with negative labels such as 'aggressive', 'controlling' and 'demanding' or, God forbid, the dreaded 'bitch' label.[35]

Without doubt, women leaders are susceptible to unfair prejudice and labels – including the dreaded 'bitch' and even 'witch' label, which harks back to the Middle Ages, applied to any woman who has 'power' over men. To realise the extent of it can be shocking to say the least. To illustrate, I'd like to share a professional experience that heralded a major tipping point in my own career journey – and rattled me to my core.

The lockout that rocked a nation

On 15 August 2005, almost 90 per cent of CBC/Radio-Canada employees were locked out by CEO Robert Rabinovitch in a dispute over future hiring practices. The impact of the lockout rocked the nation. Television and radio programming ceased, except for the airing of re-runs and BBC news. For anyone who worked in the central business district of any Canadian capital city, this meant seriously considering re-routing their walk to work to avoid the angry mob of CBC employees on the picket lines – who looked ready to throw tomatoes at any passers-by who looked like management.

To describe CBC employees as enraged was an understatement. You see, a significant psychological difference exists between a strike and a lockout. In a strike, employees have control. They feel empowered and passionate about the cause. In a lockout situation, employees are literally locked out of their place of work, treated like trespassers, with some even escorted out by security. The CBC crew were so infuriated they'd even started producing their own underground podcasts to make sure the public knew their truth.

In the midst of this, late on a Wednesday afternoon in early September 2005, I received the call. CBC had summoned a representative from the firm I was working with to come up with a strategy to help deal with the fallout expected from the lockout. They'd given me 48 hours to come up with a pitch. Given the super-charged sensitivities of this situation, I sensed that this gig could be a poisoned chalice and that if I failed, my career was over.

I wasn't sure whether it was God on my side, delusions of grandeur or fool's courage that was with me that morning. Maybe the fact that I had been a cadet journalist with the Australian Broadcasting Corporation had given me instant street cred with the executive. Whatever the reason, they trusted me within minutes. By the end of the meeting, I had figured out a way to manage their workforce's return to work and deal with any emotional storms. To this day, winning the contract still feels surreal. How I managed to land one of the highest profile and politically charged cases in Canadian union history still blows my mind.

The project was a roaring success. In just three weeks, my team had rolled out the initiative in every major Canadian capital city. It was such a hit that we even made the headlines a couple of times – going from 'How to heal a bruised workplace: CBC hires consultant to soothe nerves' to 'Inspiration and renewal on the picket line'.

As it turned out, this was just in time for the return to normal operations in mid-October and the commencement of Canada's most important television show: *Hockey Night in Canada*. Given Canada's obsession with the sport, I knew that getting the program back on the air probably acted as an additional incentive to expedite a hasty resolution of the dispute.

Whatever it was that sped things along, I was happy it was over. The experience of working with the CBC executive and its 600 managers had been the most challenging and exhilarating experience of my professional career to date. It had been worth the 15-hour days, the four weeks I had spent living out of a suitcase, and the countless conversations consoling the plagued consciences of many of the executives who had *not* been thrown out on the street.

But the lockout was not without its consequences. The months of dispute and pressure had forever affected many on the executive team, who struggled with survivor guilt. Despite all the coaching support, one of the female executives had even taken her own life. This was hardly a triumphant victory for CBC, even though things had finally returned to normal.

The assignment had been gruelling psychologically, despite the satisfaction of a job well done. I couldn't help but wonder what it would be like back at the office. I imagined myself being treated like an Olympian, welcomed back on home soil after winning the gold. The organisation was about to conduct annual performance reviews, and even though it had a reputation for being notoriously cheap and an old boys' club, I believed, like Kathryn, that my work with CBC could not be ignored and that, at the very least, a pay rise was imminent.

I met with my boss at a hotel bar. He ordered us whiskies and got down to business. He gave me a few pats on the back and assured me he had big plans for my future. 'It is so good that you are a career woman', he told me in a twangy French-Canadian drawl. 'You're not like the other women in our firm who keep going off and having children. You're a valuable asset, not a liability like the rest of them.'

And then I got hit with the real story about CBC.

'We want to congratulate you on the great job you did with CBC. To be honest we asked *you* to do the pitch because we thought you were the only one crazy enough to go in there and do it. We didn't expect you to win it.'

Kick in the guts.

My reward for a job well done was a microscopic pay rise for reasons of inflation, and the promise of greatness in years to come – if, of course, I didn't go off and get pregnant.

Oh, and the whiskey was on him too.

The recognition game

I'm sure this is a story you've heard before. It's all too commonplace, no matter where you sit on the totem pole at work. From the competent administrative assistant to the flashy vice-president, it goes something like this: person A does a tremendous job and goes the extra mile. Amid turbulence and roadblocks, she surpasses her targets and succeeds, leaving others awestruck at her magnificence.

Hooray!

Then what happens? She waits and hopes that someone, somewhere, will step up and acknowledge her success and reward her. But that doesn't happen often in the real world. So many of us have been there before, left feeling undervalued, used or taken for granted. By that point, protesting, causing a ruckus and asking for more is a little too late. Nobody wants to look like a whiner.

There are lessons to be learned from this.

Let me give you another example. A colleague of mine who knows Elon Musk quite well (she was an early investor in Tesla) shared the unfiltered story with me about a salary conversation with his executive assistant Mary Beth Brown that later went viral. It went something like this. After working with him for 12 years, Mary Beth plucked up the courage to ask him to be paid on par with SpaceX's top executives, based on the work she was handling. He asked her a fair question – 'Why would I pay you that?' She was surprised by his question, and responded, 'Because I have been supporting you for 12 years'. (After all, wasn't it obvious?)

Elon replied, 'Here's what I am going to do. I am going to send you and your family on an all-expenses holiday for two weeks and I am going to do your job. When you come back, let's have another chat.'

Two weeks later, she returned and what do you think happened?

Elon let her know he didn't need her anymore and she was replaced with someone else. (According to Elon, he offered Mary Beth another position at the company. She declined the offer by never showing up at the office again.)

Are you shocked? You shouldn't be. Knowing your value and being able to articulate and sell it is critical to getting ahead and staying there.

> *Waiting for recognition – and the financial rewards that come with that – doesn't set you up for success and is a demeaning position to be in.*

Too often, women have a tendency to wait to be seen and heard. It reminds me of the much-loved Charles Dickens character of orphan boy Oliver Twist, standing with his empty bowl asking for another serve of gruel - but at least he asked! Waiting for recognition - and the financial rewards that come with that - doesn't set you up for success and is a demeaning position to be in.

So, what can you do instead?

- *Make your value visible*: Counting on people to spot your talent and give you a pass upward is naive.
- *Manage your own career*: Take the matter into your own hands and steer your career in the direction you want it to go in.

- *Set the terms:* Negotiate prior to engaging in a high-risk task or assignment that comes with high rewards.
- *Own it:* Set your boundaries and own your agenda.
- *Command respect:* People will respect you more when you are confident and clear about what you want.

Are women ineffective as leaders?

The sad reality is that the experience I had with my boss happens way too often (maybe not with a whiskey in hand). The psychological position is clear on this. A deep-rooted belief exists that women are less effective leaders than men. In more traditional cultures, like with my employer back in 2005, this belief continues to be an even greater contributing factor to the gender gap in leadership.

Here's another true story you're going to enjoy – brace yourself!

The organisers of an all-staff conference for senior people at Ernst & Young in 2018 explained the differences in leadership effectiveness between genders by the size of their brains and the way they take in information. Female leaders were told that their 'brains were 6 per cent to 11 per cent smaller than men's'. They were also advised:

Women's brains absorb information like pancakes soak up syrup so it's hard for them to focus. Men's brains are more like waffles. They're better able to focus because the information collects in each little waffle square.[36]

With this kind of belief system underpinning the culture at Ernst & Young, it's not hard to extrapolate why a little over 20 per cent of Ernst & Young's partners are women, and why accounting firms in general lack women in senior roles across the industry.

A lot can be learned from the Ernst & Young journey (and I know that they have been working hard to address these issues). It's a great example of what is being called out as 'brilliance bias'. In her book *Invisible Women: Exposing Data Bias in a World Designed for Men*,

Caroline Criado Perez shares the results of a study into male and female professors and their perceived effectiveness as teachers. An analysis of over 14 million reviews on the website RateMyProfessors. com found that female professors are more likely to be voted as 'mean', 'unfair', 'strict' and 'annoying'. Male professors were described as 'brilliant', 'intelligent', 'smart' and 'genius'. As Criado Perez points out, 'so many female geniuses have been written out of history' because they 'don't come to mind easily'. The result is that when 'brilliance' is considered a requirement for a job, what is really meant is 'a penis'.[37]

And what about ambition? How are ambitious women being viewed?

Women who are perceived as ambitious or not seen as ambitious enough are also more likely to be penalised for their success.[38] Case in point, when asking for recognition for a job well done, I was viewed as inappropriately demanding and aggressive. I know this because Jean-François ended up doing a stint with the same company and that's how they described me to him years later!

Let's go back to the Ernst & Young example. A report that followed the training session stated that women were not 'ambitious' enough in the firm. In the same breath, women were warned not to challenge their male colleagues if they wanted to be considered for promotion.

I will leave that with you.

Now what about Kathryn Underwood, the protagonist of our leadership story from part I? She became even more vulnerable to gender bias because she was competing for a CEO role in a culture with no history of female role models at the top. The research on this is robust. Men's perceptions are more likely to influence female career outcomes in male-dominated domains such as corporate leadership and politics.[39] Kathryn was also up against a pervasive belief that women don't want really to be CEOs of companies or take on leadership roles.[40] This means the playing field was not even close to being even, right from the start.

Kathryn didn't succeed in getting the job of top dog at Kudos, but her story is a positive example of a competent leader who displayed strong professional identity and authenticity without losing herself in the process. In Sheryl Sandberg's terms, Kathryn Underwood 'leaned in', courageously pursuing her career goals with passion, confidence and fearlessness against all odds.

Her example encourages us to go against the grain, strive harder and ask for more. It also reminds us of what's possible when we do.

The lesser-known threat

Kathryn's story also exposes a lesser-known threat that is perhaps even more dangerous to women reaching for elevated professional goals (and the reason for this book). We're talking about the deliberate, subtle and sometimes fatal ways in which women actively hold other women back. At Kudos, a traditional corporate culture, the lack of female representation at the top and the mentality of other women such as Emma Darling and Susan White were treacherous obstacles for senior women wanting to get ahead.

My findings confirmed that women blocking other women in many different forms is still a very real threat to getting ahead.

In my more recent interviews with over 30 male and female global C-suite leaders across various industry sectors, I wanted to understand the current state of play. My findings confirmed that women blocking other women in many different forms is still a very real threat to getting ahead. I also uncovered that those who have had firsthand experiences, irrespective of severity, are still manifesting high levels of related anxiety and untreated post-traumatic stress. This is consistent with current research trends linking higher burnout rates and stress-related responses in women at work who are not actively seeking professional help to combat the lingering trauma.[41]

Newsflash – this is not a figment of our imagination, and we're not dealing with it. During my interviews and roundtables, a pioneering leader in the technology space shared this with me:

> *One of the worst jobs I ever had was in an all-female C-suite role and, oh my God, it was the only time someone brought me to tears in my entire professional life. I was hyperventilating going to work. I know not all women are like this, but I have a lot of friends who are being bullied by other women right now as we speak, and their stories are shocking. This needs to change.*

In my role, I like to keep the faith. I believe attitudes can be changed through the examples of powerful women and organisations providing support for women leaders popping up all around the globe. That's why acclaimed business leaders such as Sheryl Sandberg, Melinda Gates and Nicola Forrest, politicians such as former prime minister of New Zealand Jacinda Ardern and former prime minister of Finland Sanna Marin, and actors with clout such as Emma Watson (of the *Harry Potter* franchise) are pioneers of our time. They utilise their fame and fortune to raise awareness of the need for women to help other women reach new professional heights and rectify the imbalance. Even Reese Witherspoon reminds us through her film production company Hello Sunshine that 'If you want to change the stories, you need to change the storytellers'.[42] These women are trying to make a difference and represent those women who lift other women.

But there are also those who don't and that is why this book has been written.

Closer to home, as a woman in a position of power and influence, Australia's first female foreign minister, Julie Bishop, shared with me her leadership journey. Throughout her career, she has been a woman who has had a lot of 'firsts'. As such, she has always felt it her duty to open doors and create opportunities for other women. She is an emboldening example of a woman who has sought to appoint and promote qualified women to decision-making roles when given the chance.

She said,

> There were so few women either coming into politics or at senior levels.
> So, I saw it as part of my responsibility to make it easier for another
> woman to follow me, not harder, and I set out to do that throughout
> my political career. I would always make it a conscious effort to make
> it easier for women to follow me.

But let's go back to my story for a moment, which is one of triumph not despair. Of rise, not fall. My experience fuelled where I took my career next.

To this day, I see myself as someone who has been supported by countless inspiring and powerful women and men over the years, which continues today.

So, what happened after that unexpected performance review in a downtown Montréal bar? Louise, the managing director from one of Canada's top-tier human capital companies, heard of my work on the CBC gig and gave me a call. She didn't want to tear me down. She wanted to find out more about the person who had ripped the contract out from under her elite organisation with an impressive portfolio of famous clients they never expected to lose.

Two months later, I was looking out the window of my new office in Ottawa, marvelling at the view of the snow-dusted parliament buildings and planning the future as 'leader of the opposition'.

Real talk: if all female leaders were like Sheryl, Melinda, Nicole, Jacinta, Sanna, Emma, Reese, Julie and Louise, this book would not be necessary.

What it takes to succeed

I am often asked by leaders to describe the characteristics that enable successful women to 'part the Red Sea' and move into the upper echelons of influence. No easy answer to that question is possible, but here's what I tell them. Women who make it into higher-order positions display a dominance of the following characteristics: roaring courage, unshakeable self-confidence (most of the time, they are infallible), a strong sense of justice, a burning desire to be in control of their own destinies, and the unreasonably ambitious belief that they will get there.

A study published by Princeton University concluded that successful women leaders also demonstrate critical attributes including resilience, energy and empathy – all of which are needed for success on a path full of resistance and difficulty as women face stereotype threat, barriers and other unique challenges, such as finding a work-life balance.[43]

But how do you stay the course when tested against the odds?

In the cutthroat world of politics, Julie Bishop offered a fabulous insight into how she has managed to stay on her path without going off the rails, or melting into a puddle like Kathryn. Used to being the only woman in the room and having to deal with a barrage of critique and judgement over many years during her political career and beyond, she told me:

Criticism is fine if it's from a source you respect, a person whose judgement you might listen to, or whose perspective means something to you. Block the criticism from the white noise, life is too short.

Her advice?

Get it out of your life. Go and have a shower. Stand in the shower, shut your eyes and drain all the negativity. Watch it washing down the drain. Then get out of the shower.

In the next chapter, I delve into the biological roots underpinning female aggression at work. Some prevailing views argue women fighting women at work is just part of how women are hard-wired. But is there any truth to this?

Chapter 18

It's (still) all
about sex

The day will come when men will recognize woman as his peer, not only at the fireside, but in councils of the nation. Then, and not until then, will there be the perfect comradeship, the ideal union between the sexes that shall result in the highest development of the race.

Susan B. Anthony

Believe it or not, Kathryn's story from part I sheds light on a phenomenon that is age-old. We know that women who mistreat other women in the workplace can often do so in unforgivable ways, yet it is usually swept under the carpet and dismissed.

But how is it that some women can be so nasty? What is it that propelled Susan White and Emma Darling to behave so badly? Is it a female thing?

Looking to our closest relatives

Some of the answers to these questions might be found in Charles Darwin's theory of evolution. I spoke to Andrew O'Keeffe, author of *Hardwired Humans: Successful Leadership Using Human Instincts*, to gain a new perspective from the animal kingdom. He shed some light on the issues through the research he's been doing with Dr Jane Goodall on chimps in captivity.

Apparently, during mating season at Taronga Zoo in Sydney, Australia, the primates are frisky as hell and the female chimpanzees jostle to get as much action as possible. Andrew told us that one of the chimps he'd been observing, Sally, got pregnant, while another chimp, Josie, did not. After Sally had her baby, Josie was so distraught over her failure to conceive that she turned her anger on Sally's infant and tried unsuccessfully to kill it. Several months later, Josie conceived and had a baby. But Sally still carried a grudge for what Josie had tried to do and in a violent act of retribution, she killed Josie's baby.

This true story of vengeful female chimp behaviour is a poignant example of the lengths female primates take to hurt and punish other females in their community who have wronged them. Apparently, this behaviour is at its worst at the time of oestrus, the state preceding ovulation in most mammals, when female chimp aggression forces even the most magnanimous of alpha males to duck for cover.

O'Keeffe's book takes a big leap and provides us with an interesting analysis of the primate world to help explain some of *Homo sapiens'* workplace antics and demystify human behaviours. It begs the question: is being bitchy part of our DNA, or are women behaving badly towards other women because of a conscious choice they make? And why compare us to chimps at all?

O'Keeffe explains that it makes sense to draw comparisons because chimps are the socio-species closest to humans. Just like in the workplace, the primate world has a hierarchical structure that provides the framework for social standing. Among chimps, female primates who are more influential will often bully and socially ostracise females of lower ranking.

So, how do lower-level female chimps rise in the primate ranks? It appears that the size of their genitals makes the difference. The more engorged and swollen a female's genitals, the more attractive they become to the male chimps – so much so that chimps with the enhanced private parts go from being bullied by the other females to become coveted by the males in the tribe and protected from harm.

It seems in the chimp world at least, it really is all about sex. But what about for us humans?

Hierarchy, scarcity and the social order

In our modern-day workplaces, where women are under-represented at the upper echelons of power, one might expect some female primal instincts to kick in. If this assumption is true, it holds that women are likely to engage in hyper-competitive behaviours in the face of scarce resources. With all the female tokenism and limited leadership opportunities available to women, the notion that organisational 'power' is perceived as a scarce resource is realistic. With limited leadership positions 'reserved' for women – the perceived 'right balance' – women can believe they are only competing with other women, rather than other men in leadership roles.

Perhaps we're not that different from our fellow chimps. In the animal world, about the focus is on procreation and survival. In the human world, it's about obtaining power, prestige and the 'right to vote'.

> *In the animal world, about the focus is on procreation and survival. In the human world, it's about obtaining power, prestige and the 'right to vote'.*

In an interview with the much-respected CEO of a state sporting organisation, he had this to share:

> In female sport teams it can be a very competitive environment where there is intense jealousy among players. In any elite sport for men or women it can be hard to see teammates succeed ahead of you which causes disharmony reduces collaboration and increases conflict.

This view was echoed in a recent episode of *The Imperfects* podcast. Hosts Hugh van Cuylenburg, Ryan Shelton and Josh van Cuylenburg were interviewing seven-time world champion surfer Layne Beachley, and I was fascinated to hear about her experiences in and out of the water. She said,

> Being on tour was sometimes soul destroying. There were moments when I felt like I belonged and when I didn't. I belonged when I was losing, and I didn't when I was winning. Women's surfing has a real scarcity mentality. We dragged each other down; we beat each other up.

I brought the competition out of the water and got into their heads to unravel them.

Her experiences echo the sentiments of a female CEO from the technology sector who told me:

When women support each other in teams, you see the best of the best; when they don't, you see the worst of the worst. Female 'hot house' environments take it next level.

Not a lot of research exists on intrasexual competition between females; however, what data is available provides some interesting food for thought. In the quest for finding a mate, two competitive strategies that are most typically used by women in the face of perceived 'resource scarcity' are self-promotion and what's called 'derogation of rivals'.[44]

Self-promotion involves women trying to make themselves more attractive – for example, by wearing make-up and tight-fitting clothes. Derogation of rivals is about using indirect aggression to reduce the perceived mate value of a rival. The most common tactics include spreading rumours about the rival's fidelity and/or promiscuity, disparaging her appearance (for example, slut and fat shaming), excluding her from her peer group, or giving her the dreaded silent treatment.[45] For some females, this can also include tactics like power-dressing, and pointing out their own achievements in comparison to others' flaws.[46]

As you can see, even if we're not talking about sex or the search for love, tactics some women use to bully other women are persistent. That's why movies like *Mean Girls* have risen in popularity over recent years (there is even a musical remake!): they represent something very real happening in our everyday experience that has a massive impact on the way women learn to manage these situations later in life. And for the most part, they are not managed well.

Was Emma Darling justified in doing to Kathryn what could be deemed to come naturally? She spread rumours to destroy her reputation and so increase her value in the eyes of her prospective mate, Preston Steele, and gain his favour. Did Emma have a choice in how she behaved, or were her natural instincts just far too strong? Even if you believe the evolutionary rationale, is the urge to take each other down just too hard to resist?

God help you if you're good looking

Adding good looks into the mix of female relationships can also add another layer of complexity – so much so, that researchers have found that females both want attractive friends to improve their chances of male attention, while at the same time can feel threatened by their friends' good looks.[47]

Compelling evidence also suggests that women who are perceived as good looking are more likely to be punished by other women. This is because in the workplace, sex is often used as a weapon to get ahead or a driver to quash another. Social scientists Roy Baumeister and Jean Twenge provide an explanation for this, discussing a double standard of sexual morality that exists in which women 'stifle each other's sexuality because sex is a limited resource that women use to negotiate with men, and scarcity gives women an advantage'.[48]

So here we are again, back to basic primitive brain antics.

In an illuminating Canadian study, psychologists Tracy Vaillancourt and Aanchal Sharma put this belief to the test. They manipulated participant perceptions to test whether women behaved more nastily toward a sexily dressed woman versus a conservative-looking woman. The result? Participants laughed, ridiculed and rolled their eyes at the sexily dressed woman while, in contrast, didn't react at all to the same woman dressed more conservatively.[49] This finding is consistent with evidence that women are threatened by, disapprove of, and punish women who appear too sexy by means of indirect aggression.

What's more, women reported being less likely to be friends with the sexy woman, because the perceived perception for them to potentially steal their man was high.

How does all this play out in the workplace for women? Does adding a bit of sexiness to the mix assist or stifle a woman's career progression? To answer this question, let's turn to the world stage for real-life examples.

In 2012, Melissa Nelson, a 33-year-old dental assistant from Iowa, was fired by her boss, James Knight (after working for him for 10 years) for being too attractive. The Iowa State Supreme Court ruled that Knight acted legally in firing Nelson because he - and his wife - viewed her as a threat to their marriage. The (all male) court ruled 7-0 that bosses can fire employees they see as an irresistible attraction, even if they have not engaged in flirtatious behaviour or otherwise done anything wrong.

In a follow-up interview, Nelson also shared that her boss had considered her a stellar worker, but in the final months of her employment, he had complained that her tight clothing was distracting, once telling her that 'if she saw his pants were bulging, she would know her clothing was too revealing'.

Then there was Debrahlee Lorenzana. In 2010, Lorenzana lost her job at Citibank - because, she alleged, her good looks made her co-workers feel uncomfortable.

At that unforgettable Ernst & Young training session I mention in chapter 17 (lest we forget), women were advised to 'dress fit and not provocatively' while refraining from addressing men face-to-face if they wanted to progress in the firm.

But wait, there is more.

Our own Australian Defence Force has published a gender guide for handling 'hot warrior women'. Soldiers being lectured on gender awareness defined female recruits as 'Xena personalities' and setting 'sexual chemistry guidelines' during induction week as part of their army safety training.[50] The document states:

The Army should aim to be the home of 'Xena' personalities. Don't be scared of Xena, enable her and get out of the way.

Apparently, the document, called a 'gender guide', was formulated 'to prepare the military for the coming era of gender equality' as the army attempts to build a preventative strategy by signalling to men that charismatic female personalities are not sexual objects, nor threats, but *just* leaders, and therefore they should 'calm down and treat her as such'.

No doubt this is a fumbling attempt at doing the 'right' thing but at least their hearts are in the right place.

These examples demonstrate the quandary good-looking women are placed in by both sexes and in different industries. Being attractive will often help you get in the door, but it might not help to keep your job. And if you're in the Defence Force, it could lead to a test of your ability to deal with sexual chemistry and awkward scenarios.[51]

Fight the urge to be mean

At the end of the day, the onus is on all of us to take control over the way we behave. Whether you like or dislike another woman, it doesn't warrant the cattiness and cruel treatment so often served up.

Bringing our unconscious instincts to consciousness awareness might just be the answer to women being better able to manage their biases toward other women and suppress those raging inner demons.

It's time to change the course on these behaviours and fight the urge to be mean. Part of the answer lies in becoming more aware. Bringing our unconscious instincts to consciousness awareness might just be the answer to women being better able to manage their biases toward other women and suppress those raging inner demons.

The sisterhood stitch up

The sisterhood is not okay. But it's not just women who are work colleagues or unknown women you've never met that present as threats (that's a whole other book!). Jean-François and I often receive calls for help from women suffering from one of the more devastating acts of psychological trauma that takes the experience to a whole other level – being betrayed by another woman within an existing trusted relationship.

Jessica, a leader from the pharmaceutical industry, described it to me like this:

> I had a best friend at work, and we bonded over our shared work experiences (getting through, overcoming a bad boss, succeeding and so on). We confided in each other, shared our aspirations, dreams and struggles – the whole nine yards! Then, one day, something shifted. Maybe it's because we were getting too close. I couldn't help measuring myself against her and vice versa. When it was time for a promotion, we wished each other good luck and hugged. But it was all phony, and I later learned that she got the job by talking behind my back. In hindsight, the green-eyed monster had taken over and reason walked out the door, taking our years of friendship with it.

We hear examples like this often, and know all about the lengths to which some people will go to get ahead – even if it means sacrificing a 'friendship' in the process.

It's a well-known occurrence that closeness with someone from the same sex breeds comparison. Comparison tends to breed envy, jealousy and, ultimately, the drive to act on those feelings. It's the shadow side of human relationships that is all too common, and at the root of psychological trauma for too many.[52]

From a psychological point of view, these behaviours go back a long way and are potentially rooted in existing rivalries with siblings (for example, dealing with an older sister who put you down or a younger sister who used her 'being the youngest' card to undermine you every time she got a chance).

Whether it's your sibling, a friend, a close colleague or your boss, being mistreated or not helped by other woman in life or at work tends to hurt more – perhaps because we expect more from our female friends and peers. And it will always feel worse if the mistreatment comes from someone we care about.

Jamila Rizvi, columnist for *Sunday Life* magazine (part of *The Sydney Morning Herald*) and deputy managing director for *Future Women*, talks about the higher social expectations women place on other women to explain why the wounds cut so deep. According to Rizvi, women expect other women to behave better so feel more disappointed when then don't.

Here's where I land on this.

The prevalence of the sisterhood paradox highlights how our organisational systems are cultivating scarcity environments where conflict between women becomes likely.

It is unlikely that women are more inherently cruel to each other than to other genders. However, the prevalence of the sisterhood paradox highlights how our organisational systems are cultivating scarcity environments where conflict between women becomes likely. As an example, academic studies and surveys back up the high incidence of negative experiences women have had working for a female boss, so much so that many prefer not to work with another woman.[53] This may be evidenced in companies with frequently high or consistent turnover among female direct reports to a female boss. Some women also believe men make better mentors and sponsors, when given the choice, due to the perception they are better connected, both internally and externally.[54]

In the next chapter, I start to identify the different types of female aggression at work – because they are not all created equal. This will help you to choose the best approach to diffuse the situation and get the best outcome for everyone involved.

Chapter 19

A bully by any other name

If you don't deal with your demons, they will deal with you, and it's gonna hurt.

Nikki Sixx

Behaving badly, being a jerk and bullying are not the same thing.

Your ability to be able to successfully deal with female aggression at work starts with understanding the differences between the various forms that come out to play, the most severe of which is bullying. This is the kind of behaviour where a female bully at work takes it to the next level, playing emotional and tormenting games. Research shows that bullying (with the intent to maim or destroy) is responsible for higher reported levels of stress and sickness among female colleagues.[55] It is also one of the undiscussable blockers to female career progression.

Recent research shows that anywhere from 46 per cent to 52 per cent of women say that they have experienced workplace bullying or harassment over the preceding three years, more than half of it by another woman.[56] And according the Workplace Bullying Institute's 2024 *Workplace Bullying Survey*, while 71 per cent of bullies were men, 18 per cent of 'worst case' situations of workplace bullying was women-on-women.[57]

Given the data, you would be right to assume that a roadmap exists to help those going through the experience to navigate the situation and not become a victim of its aftermath. In reality, very little published information exists on the topic, and this is part of the reason Jean-François and I were so spurred on to share Kathryn's story and write this book.

The word from the streets

To gather more meaningful data, Jean-François and I 'hit the streets' so to speak to seek out real-life stories from women around the world who were willing to share their struggles on the topic. In hearing these stories, what really hit home for us was how difficult it was for women who had experienced female mistreatment and bullying to move on from the experience. The devastation caused by the bullying was still palpable. Some had been energised by the experience and had, like Kathryn, come back triumphant, but they were fewer than the former.

So, why aren't women going public with this? Why isn't a very real threat to female health and wellbeing getting discussed? A recent qualitative analysis provides answers.[58] Researcher Britni Warner found that often the unexpected and covert nature of the bullying behaviours leaves them questioning if it was really happening (there's another word for this: 'gaslighting'[59]).

One of the participants in Warner's study said,

> *My first incident, I would say I was really taken aback. It was kind of a surprise, it was a strange comment and, and I was not sure how to interpret what was being said to me. As I mentioned, it was a little passive aggressive, so I wasn't sure if it was directed to me, or if it was a broad statement, or how to interpret it.*

Talking about this bad behaviour is also 'forbidden' – and on a couple of levels. Firstly, women who 'out' their sisters may be seen by other women as disloyal traitors. To illustrate, take Meredith Fuller, a psychologist for 40 years and author of the book *Working with Bitches: Identify the 8 Types of Office Mean Girls and Rise Above Workplace Nastiness*. Dr Fuller's book sparked an outrage among female critics and a spate of vicious attacks as she was seen as deepening the great divide of male and female inequality by not supporting her sisters.

On the contrary, after so many years of working with clients who commonly complained about the schoolyard-style bullying and exclusion tactics women use to get their own way at work, Dr Fuller's work provides compelling evidence to suggest how women get in their own way. Her book forces us to evaluate our own level of 'inner nasty' to become more consciously aware and defend against gender bias, rather than being part of the problem.

Secondly, what makes aggressive antics difficult to discuss is that women who are seen to protest or confront the perpetrators risk being perceived as petty, overemotional or high maintenance by others in the workplace. Research demonstrates that women who have had interpersonal difficulties with a female co-worker are viewed more negatively than men and will most likely be overlooked for future career opportunities. Moreover, women involved in female–female conflict hold grudges and are less likely to work productively in the future.[60]

Women who are seen to protest or confront the perpetrators risk being perceived as petty, overemotional or high maintenance by others in the workplace.

An example that springs immediately to mind is a client of mine, who I'll call Monica. Just six months after she was ambushed by a female peer and unjustifiably lost the trust of many of her colleagues, Monica was still reeling. She did not fight back or quit her job, even though her working situation had become unbearable. She went silent. Every day at work was like Groundhog Day, going through the motions in a zombie-like state just to get to 5 o'clock. She figured it was better to hide than to create waves and get punished for it. She had mentally checked out.

What eventually kicked her out of her slump was the realisation that she was getting a dose of some serious karma. You see, Monica had also been guilty of mistreating other women. It wasn't until the shoe was on the other foot that she realised the full impact of her actions. 'Being honest about how guilty I felt about being horrible to other women is a place we all need to go if we are to change,' she told us.

For Monica, only when she was on the receiving end of a female-led attack was she able to take stock of her own inner biases toward other women.

Light bulb on.

Time to stand up and speak out

The label 'bully' has become weaponised in the working world. Indeed, it is often used to name a plethora of behaviours, some of which couldn't be further from what it actually is to be a bully. Add the word 'female' in front of it and you have a double-edged sword of pain.

This is why, in writing this book, I anticipated a backlash from female colleagues, friends and strangers. As I've mentioned earlier in the book, I was getting ready to dodge a barrage of rotten tomatoes, much like Dr Meredith Fuller had after the publication of her book *Working with Bitches*. To road-test the content, I accepted an invitation from a national Australian association for women to give a talk on the subject to their members. I was expecting the worst. Many women Jean-François and I had discussed the subject matter of the previous edition with had been appalled that we had even written it. They seemed disgusted at its mere mention, and worried about how it could set us back in the gender equality arena.

Women are often faced with a choice: shut up and suck it up, or tell the truth and be damned for it.

Prior to the event, I was scolded. 'How dare you stigmatise women as being bitchy!' some said, while others believed our book would 'only fuel those women-haters out there!' Others took offence at our use of the term 'bitch' in the first edition, arguing that it had a negative connotation and only served to highlight 'women's inhumanity to other women'.[61]

These comments echo the idea of the sisterhood paradox – that is, that women are stereotypically portrayed as caring, compassionate and relationship-oriented, and when they deviate from this expectation, they are severely penalised. This means women are often faced with a choice: shut up and suck it up, or tell the truth and be damned for it.[62]

But, it turned out, the women who were appalled by my focus on female bullying were in a minority. I walked into a sold-out auditorium of almost 100 women who were highly engaged by what I had to say. I didn't face any anger or defensiveness, and there was not a tomato in sight. Instead, something amazing happened. The participants bonded over this topic that had left many of them with very real pain and anxiety during their careers. Individuals stood up in succession to share their stories and seek coaching and support from the others in the group to help work through the female aggression and bullying scenarios they had to manage. The healing in the room was palpable. This was the closest we had seen to what a truly supportive women's club might look like, and what it would feel like to be part of; it was powerful.

What came from the group was a crucial need to understand how female-on-female fighting equates to the insidious and sometimes fatal form of bullying I am focused on exposing. And I say 'insidious' because it is so often invisible to others. So how do you identify what a female bully really looks like and distinguish her from the everyday mean girl? In the next section, I help you to spot the difference and recognise what's happening.

The worst kind of psychological bullying

Most people have a pretty sound intuitive idea of what bullying is and of what kind of behaviours are used to express it. However, I've found a significant number of ambiguities and myths remain involved in its comprehension; therefore, it's worth providing some clarification.

Let me be clear: what I am describing in this book is a phenomenon that goes way beyond women snubbing or being cold towards one another. I am talking about the worst kind of bullying – one that is defined in the following way:

> A destructive process consisting of a succession of hostile statements and/or actions which, if taken in isolation, may seem more or less harmless, but whose constant repetition have pernicious and devastating effects.[63]

In the context of this book, I'm focusing on the bullying unleashed by women onto other women. Real, legitimate bullying is not a one-time occurrence. It is a pattern of behaviours and/or a series of incidents that takes place frequently and over time. These bullying tactics are 'repeated verbal or psychological attacks or intimidations that are intended to cause fear, distress or harm to the victim'.[64] Note the word 'intend'. If this were a criminal trial, all the prosecution would have to prove to have someone incarcerated is they have displayed *mens rea* (an intention of wrongdoing), not whether they had succeeded. You can see where I am going with this.

In the work context, bullying is defined as 'harassing, offending, socially excluding someone, or negatively affecting someone's work tasks'.[65] Psychological bullying behaviours are considered forms of direct (obvious) and indirect (subtle) aggression. Tactics range from intimidation, verbal threats and constant criticism, to deliberately undermining a person's work, setting someone up to fail and spreading rumours, to name a few. Bullying can also be about committing acts of commission (doing things to others) or omission (withholding resources from others) and exclusion from participation (this includes social ostracism).[66]

What distinguishes bullying in the workplace from better-known and widely reported microaggressions? The description in the literature describes characteristic phases that build up over time to achieve the desired outcomes.

Here's a rundown of these phases to help you identify whether you have become the target of a bully at work.

Phase 1: Fault finding and criticism

In this first phase, the targets of bullies are exposed to frequent fault-finding and criticism. At the same time, they report repeated attempts to undermine their position, status, worth, value and/or potential.[67] This psychological battering is likely to cause a feeling of isolation. Typically, targets may then withdraw and disengage from work to manage the psychological issues that are beginning to appear. The target's self-confidence is already taking a beating.

Phase 2: Target is singled out and treated differently from others

Constantly under the microscope, the target cannot get away with anything. Worst yet, their responsibilities increase but their area of control or influence shrinks as they are squeezed from all sides and corners. At this stage, the decline in performance becomes obvious and the target can no longer cope with the unrealistic demands of the job. While resilience is seen as a protective factor to help the target weather the bullying storm, it is not an infinite resource, and eventually performance starts to suffer.[68] The target starts to crumble.

Phase 3: Twisted and misrepresented

In this final phase, the target finds that everything they say is twisted around and misrepresented. The trap has been laid out and they have no more room to manoeuvre. The bully is in control, waiting for the final blow to eliminate the victim once and for all. It's game over!

You can see how important it is to be able to recognise the early warning signs of bullying. Being prepared to take action before you're too caught up in the web that's been spun is key to remaining buoyant and outsmarting the bully – before your self-esteem is in tatters and you have no energy left to fight.

Rise of the 'Queen Bee'

At a fundamental level, the high incidence of gender and status inequality still seen in modern workplaces has (not surprisingly) created fertile soil for the emergence of women known as 'queen bees'. Queen bees are typically personified by ambitious women wanting to maintain their power in their jobs and get ahead. You only have turn to characters such as Miranda in the Hollywood blockbuster *The Devil Wears Prada* and even Alexis Colby in *Dynasty* to see stereotypical female bullies in action. These are women who have succeeded but who not only refuse to help other women do the same but also actively prevent them from doing so.

More specifically, the 'Queen Bee Syndrome' is a phenomenon defined in the early 1970s as highly successful women who have reached the top of their game but are regarded as even more sexist and ruthless that their male counterparts. Queen bees usually distance themselves from other females who they perceive as competition, refuse to assist them and block their rise up the ranks.

Our Susan White (from part I) is a great example of a queen bee in action. She was committed to blocking Kathryn's success in the role, despite her being the better candidate. Mrs White perceived Kathryn's presence at the executive table as a social threat diminishing her own power and status.

Finally, in the world of business, with few female role models at the top and higher positions for women in leadership remaining more elusive than customary, female aggression tactics are more prolific. Look closely in the media and you're soon overwhelmed by stories of workplace bullying, gender discrimination and even tragic accounts of people taking their own lives because of their inability to fight back against abusive behaviour experienced at work.

Consider a recent story shared by a senior male leader in the resources sector. He described a general manager who asked his female office manager to conduct a 'Hunger Games' to hire new recruits, putting potential personal assistants through a series of tough trials to see who was the fastest in typing up notes. The contestant who 'survived' was offered the position with the firm. This behaviour, though extreme, is not uncommon in the workplace.

At the end of the day, what is clear is that instead of women supporting one another at work, a dog-eat-dog situation is still often occurring where only the toughest survive. Yes, the office nasties still seem to get ahead and, yes, often the bully is promoted. The phrase 'nice girls finish last' was coined for a reason: because it's often true. Nice girls can often be taken advantage of, with their kindness mistaken for weakness. However, in the grand scheme of things, there are no real winners – only survivors waiting for the next round of fighting.

Scientists argue that perhaps what perpetuates this behaviour is the degree to which a workplace culture or industry is male-dominated and sexist. In other words, a male-dominated environment may incite female-on-female bullying and fighting. Research shows that some women have internalised a 'hazing' mentality from having to fight so hard to succeed earlier in their careers. At the end of the day, despite our human appearance, we are still animals competing for scarce resources and feeling under threat in a world perceived as having limited opportunities for women to advance.

Despite our human appearance, we are still animals competing for scarce resources and feeling under threat in a world perceived as having limited opportunities for women to advance.

It seems that the world of work has created arenas where sometimes only the fittest – and nastiest – survive. But there are ways you can recover and move on from a bully.

Moving on from a bully's attack

As trained psychologists, Jean-François and I have helped countless women who have been on the receiving end of a female bully move on with their lives. While no perfect recipes exist for a successful intervention, a few pointers are worth underlining as the first steps in the road to recovery.

Find someone who listens to understand

The first place to start is to find someone willing to listen and try to understand your experience. This can take a while. You need to feel comfortable, and this doesn't work if you haven't established trust. Be prepared for your stories to get mixed up, hesitations to creep in, an excessive rationalisation of what happened and even feelings of guilt. You may even have sudden bursts of self-blame, and say things like, 'I'm probably overreacting', 'It's not that bad', Don't worry, I'll get over it!' or 'I am just being emotional'.

Be patient

Be patient and respect your own rhythms and defence mechanisms. I wish it were an easier process but working through an experience like this inevitably comes with a few potential pitfalls along the way. To illustrate, when Jean-François and I saw Kathryn months after her ordeal, she was living as a recluse and shattered. At first, she simply needed to vent, and we were her sounding board, often staying quiet. Our efforts to help her were met with moderate success, but this venting was a necessary step in her healing journey. Just starting to talk about what happened and confronting the reality of what happened is always the first step on the road to recovery – seeing the world as it is, not as you wish it to be.

Work through self-blame and feelings of betrayal

Kathryn struggled to articulate what had happened to her, and make sense of her experience. The psychological blockers that stunted her path to recovery were self-blame and anger. She blamed herself for everything that had gone wrong. She felt like a failure. She was angry with herself for not reading the play better, for allowing herself to be bullied. She was angry with everyone else for their subterfuge, for the emotional abuse, and for the lack of support and belief in her. We had to help her work through these feelings before she could move on to a better place.

Working with Kathryn, it was obvious that it was not one person who had been the catalyst for her sadness. What stood out was her deep resentment toward Susan White and the treatment she'd endured at her hands during her time at Kudos. This wounding was much more deeply felt. Susan had been her mentor; Emma had not.

Reframe the experience

Kathryn needed to take the time to talk through her emotions and work things out in her mind. While Kathryn talked, our supporting role evolved, and we became more like jazz musicians. We improvised on the themes and moods that emerged, switching between quiet listening, reconstruction, reformulation, pushing back and refocusing, all with the goal of having her take stock of what had happened. She needed a fresh perspective to be able to take greater control of her next steps.

We couldn't sort out every last detail of her story, and plenty remains a mystery to us – for example, Susan White's motives, the role Kathryn had played in some of the precipitating events and why she could not help repeating some old patterns of behaviours. However, the point was not to reach the absolute truth and figure everything out. The objective was for Kathryn to have enough clarity to move on.

Shut the door and move on

One of the most difficult things to do in life is to move on from unfinished business without closure. Yet sometimes, for our own sanity, we just need to get on with life – without things being wrapped with a neat little bow. Kathryn needed to move on from this experience. She needed to turn her back on the past to move forward.

I remember an experience I had when I was trying to grapple with going through a rough divorce to my university sweetheart. I flew to Northern Thailand to spend some time at a Buddhist monastery in Chiang Mai. I was struggling to jump back into life with a more positive attitude. One of the monks shared the following story with me that really helped to jolt me out of the slump I was in:

> *You need to imagine yourself standing at a doorway with a big, heavy suitcase. The threshold of the doorway represents your current life. The suitcase represents your past. To move into the future, you must drop that suitcase behind you, walk through the door and slam it shut. Leave the past in the past. Don't let your past become an anchor around your neck. Move forward into the sun, into your future, and don't look back or try to open the door again.*

We asked Kathryn to stand up, pass through the threshold of her present and walk into the future of the life she wanted and never look back.

Avoid the victim trap

Kathryn managed to whip herself back in shape in record time. Overall, 12 months isn't long to work through the emotions, stress and trauma that go hand in hand with an experience like hers and come back on top. But it isn't always like that and can really depend on the person you are working with. Everyone bounces back differently and in their own time. There is no right or wrong. What can slow down recovery, though, is having a victim mindset.

Falling into the victim trap can sound something like, 'I was screwed!' or 'This woman had it in for me!' or 'I'm the victim here!' Jean-François and I know as psychologists that if you hold on to this self-talk for too long, your recovery won't happen fast, if at all.

Acknowledging what happened and not feeling guilty about it is part of the recovery process – and a great place to start.

Playing the victim is a treacherous path to take and if you feel yourself going that path, we urge you to proceed with caution – it's very often that people can become immobilised, unable to move into a constructive and optimistic space and enjoy life again. Acknowledging what happened and not feeling guilty about it is part of the recovery process – and a great place to start. Playing the victim for a little bit is also part of the healing process, but don't stay there too long – or you risk getting stuck there forever.

Speak your truth

The same principles hold true for those who include in their recovery process the act of naming what they went through, be it psychological harassment, bullying, emotional abuse, incivility or workplace violence.

Being able to articulate and name your truth is a crucial part of the legitimising and healing process. The danger is the label can become a psychological handcuff. By handcuff, I mean that you define yourself only by that label. Truly moving on also means breaking away from these shackles.

Seek professional help

Working through this with a trained mental healthcare professional is advisable. If possible, it makes sense to start by inquiring about services your company has to offer to support employees going through tough times. Before sharing, try not to tell your stories from a purely emotional angle. You need to have sufficient facts gathered and be able to share them calmly without sounding dramatic and overly emotional.

Most organisations are usually ill-prepared to deal with bullying and may tend to water down any given conflict and/or see it as a personality clash where both sides are to blame. If you've been taken down hard, you don't need a mediator – you need the law to be on your side. Check your organisation's anti-bullying policies as well to see where you stand. Bottom line: if you feel too banged up and uncertain, it may be better to ask for external help first, if only to help you sort things out.

In the next chapter, I blow the lid on the next level of bullying – dealing with a psychopath at work. Being able to recognise who you are dealing with is critical if you want to plan an approach that prevents you getting caught in their crosshairs.

Chapter 20

Enter the psychopath

I'm not a psychopath – I'm wearing a tie!

Seth Godin

Research shows that around 5 per cent of leaders are psychopaths. To put this into context, experts estimate that around 1 per cent of all people are psychopaths and that leadership roles hold a special attraction for such individuals.[69] To give this another spin, one out of every 20 leaders passing through any given company is not the kind of person you would want as your boss. When you view this through a four-to-nine-year lens (the average length of tenure for CEOs in Australia) and the even slower rate at which organisations tend to move out their executive, this number becomes quite significant.

Psychopaths are also well known for being prone to bullying others – as well as lying, cheating and generally causing mayhem to achieve their own agenda. Psychopathology is not considered a mental health disorder despite the destructive impact of it. From a workplace perspective, evidence suggests that female leaders with psychopathic tendencies are rated as more directive, and less trans-formational and effective, while men cut from the same neurology get rewarded.[70]

Given that up to one third of workers may be the victims of workplace bullying, and over 30 per cent of workplace bullies are women, this presents an alarming portrait of a potential offender that is more than just a mean girl (or boy). has Available data also shows that female bullies are way more likely to bully other females. Males, on the other hand, are considered equal-opportunity offenders and tend to bully males and females more or less equally.

Deep breath.

It is very probable that some female bullies might also be psychopaths.

This is an alarming revelation for such an underplayed and under-represented phenomenon in the world of work that no-one talks about, wouldn't you say?

Bully versus nasty girl: How to spot the difference

What kind of person is capable of bullying someone else? I pondered this question in writing this book, along with the following: can anyone be a bully? The short answer is that it does often take a specific psychological make-up to be a serial bullying offender. As human beings, we are all capable of being mean on occasion. But to repeatedly plot, scheme and intend to psychologically destroy someone else is an entirely different ballgame. It is critical to be able to distinguish between the two behaviours.

As human beings, we are all capable of being mean on occasion. But to repeatedly plot, scheme and intend to psychologically destroy someone else is an entirely different ballgame.

Then we add in psychopaths to the mix. A psychopath is a person who manifests amoral and antisocial behaviour. They have extreme egocentricity, and a lack of or little ability to love or show empathy or establish meaningful personal relationships.[71]

You don't need to be an expert to grasp the type of behaviours a psychopath exhibits or understand the havoc they create in the lives of the people they encounter. The truth is you are surrounded by more psychopaths than you may realise. Take a look at your daily newspapers and you'll be bombarded by descriptions of morally depraved individuals of all sorts: cold-blooded killers, predators and other emotionless nut jobs. The recent US presidential elections provide real-life data on the kind of leader who is being celebrated by the majority in that country, while also providing some insights into how dangerous the likely impact will be.

Are the psychopaths at work just as bad as these larger-than-life characters in the media? In reality, only a small number of psychopaths commit the heinous crimes we so often witness on the news. The more pedestrian psychopath is not usually as overly violent, anti-social or as dramatic as what we read about.[72] While they do thrive on delusions of world domination and are compelled to abuse and humiliate others at every turn, they do not usually engage in lawless behaviours.

Bullies at work (including female bullies) often sit at the lower end of the psychopathic spectrum. They are no Jeffrey Dahmer (the US serial killer). In practical terms, this means they do not readily engage in externalised violent acts. They are instead master chameleons and covert snipers, usually with polished outward appearances and carefully managed stage effects – so much so that they blend into organisational life quite well and go undiscovered for a long time.

Other characteristics that can be used to describe psychopathic leaders are narcissistic, exploitative, charming on the surface but domineering at the core, Machiavellian (that is, using power and coercion to achieve their own agenda), conniving, thriving on chaos, skilled at bending the truth and using it to their advantage, and masterful political animals.[73]

How far would you go?

We are all capable of being a bully to some degree, without having a full-fledged personality disorder. Competitive, performance-driven and/or cutthroat environments where the law of the jungle reigns supreme naturally tend to bring out uglier behaviours in just about everybody. Specific contexts, cultures and/or authority figures can also be powerful influencers.

This was highlighted during the famous Milgram experiment from 1963. Stanley Milgram was a psychologist at Yale University who wanted to understand how far people would go in obeying an instruction, even if it involved harming another person. To do this, he conducted an experiment testing whether people could be convinced to give a punishment (an electric shock) to other individuals, if instructed to do so by someone they perceived as an authority figure. The results were shocking (pardon the pun).

Most of the participants, under direct instruction, administered up to 450 volts of electricity to those who gave the wrong answers. Milgram's experiment demonstrated how ordinary people would follow orders given by an authority figure, especially those they recognised as morally right, or based on a legal rationale. Participants were also prepared to punish perceived offenders if the authority figure promised to take the blame for the punishment they would inflict on others. Milgram held that the reactions he witnessed were ingrained in people from their upbringing, which they then brought into the workplace. Milgram's experiment serves as a startling reminder of how even good people with the best of intentions can be convinced to perform acts conflicting with their personal conscience and inflict harm on others.

Another factor in workplace bullying and psychopathic behaviour is that the aggressed commonly becomes the aggressor.

Female workplace aggression and bullying is, at its very core, still about exercising power and domination, usually with career advancement in mind.

Think about the victims of domestic violence, schoolyard bullying and other forms of abuse. Extensive psychological research shows that victims will frequently become the perpetrators of the very act that caused them so much pain.[74]

Even with these reminders, however, many differences exist between regular people and psychopaths. At a low-end level, these differences are based purely on control. When it's all said and done, female workplace aggression and bullying is, at its very core, still about exercising power and domination, usually with career advancement in mind.

In a 'dog-eat-dog' world, where competition and perceived scarcity is at the fore and only the tough survive, all of us are tested daily. As an example of this, a female senior IT executive I worked with, who had a reputation of mistreating other women, told me the following: 'I did what I had to do. Don't blame the player, blame the game.'

It's time to change the game, wouldn't you agree?

How do you spot a psychopath at work?

I'm hoping I've convinced you that the incidence of workplace psychopathology, particularly in successful leaders, is a relatively frequent occurrence. Much like the occurrence of women mistreating other women (the essence of this book), it is a phenomenon that is frequent, and not yet adequately addressed in the research, particularly in Australia.

For Kathryn, more than a few adversaries blocked the yellow brick road to her Oz, and each manifested potential psychopathological characteristics. The challenge for Kathryn was in being able to distinguish between those with real psychological disturbances, bullies on a power trip, and people simply behaving badly.

In my coaching work, I spend a lot of time helping clients like Kathryn know how to handle 'snakes in suits' successfully. One of the biggest issues in being able to identify them is acknowledging they are a real and ever-present danger. I get that it might be difficult for the saner mind to understand how it is that such individuals could stay above an organisation's radar for any length of time. Yet, the answer is simple – the psychopath is a social mastermind and will often fit perfectly in a setting where influence, money and status are front and centre, and where power games are part of the daily grind. They flourish in a context where political skills, rather than competence, are keys to the top.[75]

Also referred to as 'psychopathic executives', these 'animals' will usually occupy top leadership positions in environments where many of their character traits – such as extreme competitiveness, coolness under pressure, domination and ruthless political aggression – which would otherwise be frowned upon, are freely tolerated or even celebrated – and elected to rule a nation (I alluded to Donald Trump earlier).

The acclaimed documentary *The Corporation* (2003) poignantly exposed through various case studies how an organisation, considered a legal entity, came to adopt and promote psychopath-like destructive behaviours. This example shows how psychopathology can permeate an organisation via the hiring, grooming and promoting of individuals with similar psychological make-up.

Preston Steele (from part I) fit the psychopath shoes perfectly. The problem was Kathryn did not see him coming, nor did she realise how dangerous he was. From my and Jean-François's conversations with her, she seemed to be like most naive individuals – blinded by his charisma and good looks, which had produced a kind of 'halo effect'. The halo effect is a fundamental attribute fallacy, whereby we pay attention to the positive attributes of a person and ignore any negative attributes. This means you might consider the success of a senior leader to be a result of their hard work, dedication and skill, and put any negative experiences of them down to bad luck, poor timing or low mood. The halo effect also perpetuates the 'physical attractiveness stereotype' or the 'what is beautiful is good' principle.[76] Because Preston was charming and attractive, Kathryn naturally perceived him as a good person. She was not alone in this. The halo effect around Preston was widespread, enabling him to exploit all the weaknesses and stressors that plagued Kudos, and use them to his advantage.

It is critical for you to be aware of the existence of psychopaths in the workplace and know how to manage them accordingly. Strength also comes in numbers. To overthrow these bullies, solidarity and mass support for staging a coup d'état is critical. Unfortunately, Kathryn was not knowledgeable enough about the modus operandi of the psychopath at work to be able to manage him successfully out of the business before she went for the top job.

> *To overthrow these bullies, solidarity and mass support for staging a coup d'état is critical.*

Know the other players

The world is full of slimy sociopaths like Preston Steele and social climbers like Emma Darling (also from part I). It always amazes me how many of my clients refuse to acknowledge that jerks like these are just part of everyday working life, and that learning to manage these characters is a must for anyone wanting to get ahead.

The first rule for dealing with these kinds of people is to find out everything you can about them: who they are, what makes them tick, what their motivations are and who are they connected to. Then you establish a good relationship with them. Way back in the 16th century, Machiavelli gave us sage advice when he told us to stay close to our friends and even closer to our enemies. Kathryn didn't like Preston, and so she kept her distance from him rather than forging a stronger connection. To be honest, this is a natural reaction for most of us. To really turn the situation around to our advantage, we must do that which makes us most uncomfortable – be around people we don't like or respect.

Kathryn's candidacy for the CEO role was weakened because she couldn't predict what Preston's approach would be or whose support he would have, and was unable to tug on his heartstrings for her own battle for the role given there was no emotional connection between them. This meant that Preston was singularly focused on winning the race for the top job at all costs, without a pinch of loyalty or care for how it affected Kathryn.

In my and Jean-François's coaching work with Kathryn, long before the opportunity for the CEO's role came up, we had advised her to begin to foster relationships with key stakeholders at Kudos, particularly those she had an aversion to but who could significantly impact her career goals in the long term. We went through a process of stakeholder mapping to determine how best to communicate and build key relationships in the business and externally. We also worked with Kathryn to identify whether a low, medium or high level of nurture was required to increase the quality and connection of many of these pivotal relationships.

For Preston, we advised her to find his weakness or some way in which she could be of service to him to become invaluable. After all, Kathryn was highly skilled in ingratiating herself by being of assistance. Finding some way to give him something that no-one else could to help him fulfil his motivations was a key strategy. Keeping her finger on Preston's pulse and staying close by meant that she could have more control over his impact.

Unfortunately, like many of our clients, Kathryn's dislike of Preston overrode her ability to keep him close. Imagine if she'd known how he'd gotten his job at Kudos. Imagine if she knew him so well that she could whisper in the ear of the selection panel and other executives at Kudos and sway their judgement of him so it was more in line with the truth versus what he had projected. Imagine if she'd been able to predict his strategy for winning the role so that she could trump him with her own.

To be successful as a leader, I recommend keeping your friends close, and your enemies closer.

In the next chapter, I focus on the male perspective on female in-fighting at work. I am not sure you are prepared for what is to come, so grab the popcorn and get ready for me to roll the tapes.

Chapter 21

Gender blind
and deaf

Unless you are the target, gender is one of those things that is not visible. Privilege is invisible to those who have it.

Michael Kimmel

I remember the day. I was sitting in bed sipping on my morning coffee, scrolling through the news feeds on my phone, and there it was – an article profiling former Mumbrella advertising boss Ian Perrin. In the article, he lamented about the lack of women at the top, and asked for someone, anyone, to tell him why it was so. He said,

Given that I don't have the answers probably makes me part of the problem ... If male CEOs can't understand the cause of the issue, then there is little chance of us being part of the solution. So, I would love to know why.

Yes, I know, don't switch off please! This is an important question. What is the male view on women being under-represented at the top, and are they even aware of female aggression and women-on-women bullying taking place right under their noses? Surely, they've witnessed a few incidents during their careers?

Based on the reported frequency of corrosive female antics and the lack of reported occurrences, I can only come up with three explanations:

1. Men are simply turning a blind eye to it.
2. They don't even know it is going on.
3. They are utter cowards and aren't stepping in to do something about it.

Judging by Perrin's statement, I'm guessing it was probably one of the latter. In Australia, some hard data has emerged on this, with recent studies demonstrating that 30 per cent of Australian men don't believe gender inequality in the workplace actually exists.[77] (Yes for real, now pick yourself up from the floor!) But let's go more broadly and look at what else is happening.

A few explanations for this laissez-faire vantage can be found in the literature, which holds that in general men tend to underplay women-on-women bullying. Men also hold a broader interpretation of what constitutes non-bullying behaviours, especially if the target is female.[78] Other research shows that men are more prone to consider harassment perpetrated by women as less serious or view the female victim as provocative, laying more blame on her own behaviour and choices.

Interestingly, the research highlights an engendered aspect to recognising female versus male aggression, where it was found that individuals in general were far more likely to judge a male face as aggressive than they would a female face.[79] In the workplace, this could mean that female-perpetuated bullying is considered far less threatening, and so more insignificant, than male bullying – and, therefore, not taken as seriously.

After all, it's just women catfighting. That's what they do, right?

Delving into the male psyche

Putting my theories to the test is why I interviewed over 55 senior male leaders, from across a broad range of roles and industry sectors. I wanted to gather diverse perspectives on what they think is really going on and see if I could spot any themes. Here's a sample of the comments that came back:

Yes, I've seen it happen. I have seen it happen many times. This is not based on anything scientific or anything like that, but I do feel like women are less straightforward in their attack. It is more underhanded, you know. They'll gossip somebody out of a job – that sort of thing. How do I feel about it? I don't encourage it but it is part of corporate life. If you are in a competitive setting, you will get whacked, fairly or unfairly, straight to your face or behind your back. May the best survive!
Edward F., Group COO, loyalty business.

For sure it happens! Catfight! Catfight! Now if it is a one-way assault and one party does not know what is happening ... well, it is not as entertaining. How do I feel about it? I don't feel anything. It does not concern me, I don't interfere. I fight my battles and let others deal with theirs.

Patrick S., Senior VP Finance, banking industry.

It exists for sure, but it is not a big deal for me. I guess this is because I never went with the premise that women would bond together in the first place. You understand where I'm coming from? If you go in with the idea that women would generally tend to help each other, then I guess you could be taken aback when they don't. But I never thought that. I expect them to bond when it serves them and undermine each other when they have to – just like men!

Robert F., VP Finance, retail industry.

Listen, this place is a jungle. We all act nice, but it is a jungle. So that's it. Everybody does what you describe. Women, men, young and old, it does not matter. Is it taboo? Not to me! If it was, I would not be here to discuss it with you!

Mike T., VP Marketing, gaming industry.

I would like to believe that this does not happen in my company. Maybe it does to some extent, but it is no big deal, it is little petty things, some gossip sure. I think cream always rises to the top you know. This so-called phenomenon you described, it never really blocked women to move up the ladder. Or anyway I like to think it hasn't, not on my watch anyway.

Michael E., President and CEO, pharmaceutical industry.

Yes, I've seen it happen once in a bad way. She was a colleague, and I tried to help. Not during it, but afterwards you know. I tried to comfort her and be nice. During it I did not want to get involved. It was too complicated. It was bad!

Conrad P., Executive VP and CFO, commercial real estate lender.

I've seen it for sure. I've also seen women using men to take down other women for sure. Is that part of what you are referring to? That happens often! I think most guys are willing to go with it if the reward is worth it. I've done it – I helped my current boss get rid of a woman who was a threat to her, and it got me a nice promotion and a fat bonus. It is all part of the game.

Dave K., COO, tech industry.

I'm a purist so I always try to get people to be upfront and put their cards on the table. However, I've never really made a distinction between men and women in this regard; there can be rivalry and fighting in both instances. I guess I would say that women tend to help each other out more than men, no? If you find it not to be the case, maybe I've missed it all!

Howard B., Executive and GM, aerospace and transport industry.

It is not taboo at all! Well, let me correct this; it is taboo for women to admit it! We know better!

J.C.M., Executive Search Consultant.

What you are describing here, this character of the conniving and mean woman using underhanded tactics to get her way and keep down other women ... I mean, there has been one in every soap and drama since the beginning of television! I would not say it is taboo! Maybe it is taboo for women to admit to it. But then again, men are not exactly beating down doors to proclaim their deviousness either! Why would they? You know what I mean?

Simon H., First Vice-President, investment financial institution.

Only a handful of leaders I interviewed were prepared to take a stand and talk to the real issues. Most seemed more comfortable shrugging the behaviour off from the sidelines. A minority of those I interviewed were prepared to use the conflict to their advantage to widen the chasm of gender inequality in leadership. And some described it as a 'fight to the death situation' and believed that everyone has to protect their own interests to survive in the ruthless, fast-paced and hyper-competitive world of business today.

It only matters when you've got skin in the game

I wondered what it would take to get more men to care about female aggression and bullying. Perhaps if they had more skin in the game and not caring came at a personal cost, they would be interested in taking the blinkers off. I shared with the guys I was interviewing the statistics on how many women are being bullied at work and that it goes largely unreported until it has reached breaking point. I asked them how they would feel if it were their sister, wife or daughter on the receiving end.

That woke them up, making them jump out of their chairs (not literally), like Lazarus rising from the dead. They put their gloves on, and they were ready for a fight. Here is how their tunes changed:

What you are describing amounts to intimidation, and I don't and never stand for it, whoever or whatever the reason. Women can count on me to stand by them, I'm a rock.

Kevin B., COO, automobile industry.

What do I think about it? I think it does exist and that women should be more prepared for it. I mean, it does not serve anybody any good to be naive about it. I'm personally very sensitive to this issue.
Sylvain T., Director of Human Resources, pharmaceutical industry.

I don't tolerate it, never did and never will. It has never happened here but if it had, I would be all over it for sure.

Sid R. National Sales Director, retail industry.

Now this will blow your mind. Australia's Workplace Gender Equality Agency uncovered research that male CEOs with daughters report less of a gender pay gap than CEOs without daughters.[80] This shows the power of making it personal and what can happen when men are invited in to help solve an extreme challenge. When men have lived experience and personally advocate for females, gender-blindness decreases and the commitment to finding solutions to gender equality skyrockets.

I wanted to conclude my interviews with a focus on joint problem-solving. We are all in this together, after all. I asked the interviewees with daughters to offer some words of advice to women on the giving and receiving end of an aggressive or bullying incident at work. The initial response to this request was defensive. In a stony and serious tone, the most common response was 'I haven't raised my daughter to be a bully'.

After explaining to the interviewees that wasn't what I was asking about, I said, 'How would you advise your sister, wife or daughter if you found out they were being bullied by another female at school or work?' Most of the fathers I spoke with then came up with two courses of action:

1. They hoped their daughters would ask for help and fight back.
2. They would tell their daughters not to trust anyone at work and watch their backs.

The boys' club exists for a reason

While not my intention, my asking about bullying also provoked many men to share with me their own stories about being intimidated or harassed at work. Often, men will not recognise (as explained earlier in this chapter) or admit to being bullied by women, seeing it as an admission of weakness or opening themselves up to being called a 'pussy'.[81] Many men also report not being believed because of the misguided belief that men have more power than women.

Not surprisingly, the interviewees' recollections were often very much like those recounted by the women I (and Jean-François) had met, outlining tales of despair, fighting back and learning how to play the game better. However, one element in their storytelling really stood out – how important it was to be part of the boys' club to get ahead and be protected.

By definition, the 'boys' club' refers to a group of peers, mostly informal, that exists in or out of the workplace and is used as a sounding board or a place to vent and seek advice. Being part of this informal support group, which often means hanging out at bars after work or going to cricket and football games, was acknowledged as a critical stepping stone to accessing higher levels in their organisations. Forging these relationships and gaining sponsorship for future opportunities was seen as the most powerful way to secure their position.

For the 'alphas' I talked with, no matter how tough a work situation may become, being part of the boys' club ensured the head honchos at their organisations would have their best interests at heart, and the path to greatness remained on the horizon. They just had to take the occasional few shots on the chin and have faith.

Failing to engage at an informal level is a key reason women often lack the necessary relationships required to sponsor their candidacy for higher-order opportunities.

Social research findings substantiate the important role that social support plays for those wanting to climb the corporate ladder, with men seeming more willing than women to engage in strategic networking to build these relationships.[82]

Perhaps unsurprisingly, many women demonstrate a general reluctance to do the same, and avoid social gatherings dominated by men.

Failing to engage at an informal level is a key reason women often lack the necessary relationships required to sponsor their candidacy for higher-order opportunities. This is not the only reason, of course. Social norms and traditional organisational cultures also play a part in constructing those ceilings that women bang their heads on.

As an example of this, Abby, a high-performing client, was working in a director role at one of the 'big four' global accounting firms, and was on the partner track. However, she found herself being excluded from attending a director and partner cricket match because she was female (after all, she wouldn't be interested in cricket). A newly appointed male director on the team, poached from a competitor's organisation, was invited to participate instead. Abby has since lost her support to be considered for partner and the new recruit has taken her spot. Without question, his ability to access final decision-makers in the partner fast-track process – and her inability to form these important relationships – blocked her career potential with the firm. But it had nothing to do with a lack of willingness to network on Abby's side.

These boys' club connections and support structures may be a critical factor in why men fail to notice or recognise female bullying and aggression – women simply aren't at these gatherings to talk about their experiences.

When push comes to shove, it is also a huge eye-opener to discover that women will often prefer a male mentor or sponsor over a woman. This is because men are perceived by women as having more power and influence, and women are seen as more of a threat to future career opportunities.[83] Recent research also demonstrates that when males genuinely show an interest in championing and supporting a female subordinate, they are likely to provide more than just superficial support.[84]

Earlier in the book, I talked about the backlash effect of diversity efforts and men's involvement. This has extended to men opting out of mentoring women for fear of repercussion should they inadvertently 'cross the line', leaving them either running for cover or struggling to find their voice in this 'new normal'. Many are asking 'what do I say?' and 'what do I do?' without offending anyone. This has now become a critical barrier to achieving traction, with many male leaders not really feeling part of diversity, equality and inclusion (DEI) initiatives or knowing how to navigate them. Equally, a lack of authentic buy-in from male leaders has been found to influence the limited success in all types of diversity initiatives.

The rise of women-only

Men feel protected as members of the boys' club. But what about women, where do they go to feel safe? One of the biggest barriers at the time of writing the first edition of this book was the lack of opportunities for women to network or be invited to all-male events, and the lack of a willingness to genuinely celebrate their achievements together.

How things have changed. As I look around today, there are so many gatherings for women (and men) to connect in and out of the workplace, offering the support and space to vent, seek advice and create community.

We know that for change to happen, women need to stand as one in solidarity and lift each other to rise. And, at face value, it seems like even writing about this phenomenon of female in-fighting at work might appear to be in contradiction with the existence of so many 'girls' clubs' popping up out there.

While some of these clubs are noble in their intent, however, not all of them are. Here's what the CEO of a prominent not-for-profit organisation in Australia shared with me about her experience:

There are so many women's clubs that make it hard for you to join. They're not kind, they're not sisterhood. Men would never make men go through this kind of process to be let into the club. I wish it was as easy as saying I don't want to join your club. I'm actually hoping that they won't let me in, and then I can just forget about it.

Stop the press. And this is just one example. I have countless more reminding us that while positive momentum is evident, work still needs to be done. Complacency is not an option if we want to accelerate the speed of change.

On the other side of the world, there's also the experience of Stephanie, a business developer par excellence, who told me about a star-studded women's group she had formed in Montréal. Her idea was to gather high potentials from different organisations to share best practices, exchange ideas and help each other out.

Stephanie's belief in getting these 12 high-flyers together was that it was time for women to start supporting each other, instead of being each other's stumbling blocks. She was very deliberate in the number of members she recruited for the group, telling me,

> More than 12 people and you lose control. We have enough barriers to job success. I really wanted to get a group of influential women together and see how we could change the world somehow.

The strategy of the group was to leverage the power in their positions to make decisions that would have real impact. Stephanie was successful in generating significant business from the contacts that she made in that group. The group also became a powerful force of one voice in the Montréal job market. They carried a lot of clout and had made a collective decision to work together to get hired into senior roles in one company to take it over and lead it better.

Unfortunately, from there things didn't exactly go to plan.

'We couldn't believe it', Stephanie shared with me. She went on to explain further:

> All this talk about supporting one another to make a difference was just bluster and hot air. From the beginning, we had all agreed that we were more powerful together than apart. We agreed to remove hierarchies and commit to a level playing field. And, without question, no men were allowed in the group under any circumstances.

> *Then Marie-Claude shows up to our meeting with her arm around the current CEO. I was furious. When all was said and done the CEO did hire a few of us, but we did not end up running the company or anything like that. Marie-Claude completely screwed that one up.*

Stephanie could not get over the fact that Marie-Claude had double-crossed the group to feather her own nest. What also made her see red was the fact that several of the group members were happy to accept the second-rate positions that ended up being offered to them, rather than take a shot at the bigger opportunities that had been promised.

'Too many women are socialised to accept their lot in life,' said Stephanie. 'They are too comfortable playing second fiddle and accepting the scraps that are offered. It's sad really.'

Reflecting on these accounts of two sides of the same coin, I couldn't help but think of a famous psychoanalyst I know who encouraged his students to watch English zoologist Desmond Morris's documentaries on the animal kingdom to understand human behaviour. These stories shed light on two distinct and polarising sets of human behaviours – those that bond us together for protection or divide us for domination. It is indeed a sobering realisation to acknowledge that the rules of the wild may still apply to us human animals – and extend to the concrete urban jungle that many of us call home.

A very real need exists to encourage the conscious building of networks and communities of women who are willing to provide true encouragement and assistance.

Sobering though it may be, the call to action is obvious here. A very real need exists to encourage the conscious building of networks and communities of women who are willing to provide true encouragement and assistance. Women also need not to opt out from attending male-dominated events – and instead keep our hand in the game.

Advice for the next generation

During my research, I was asked by several of the male leaders interviewed to counsel them on how to help their daughters prevent bullying attacks from other women. On reflection, some of them wondered if they hadn't underplayed such occurrences before. They asked me for advice and, while a magic formula certainly doesn't exist, I gladly gave them a few take-aways to share and discuss with their sisters, wives and daughters – which I now share with you.

Know thyself

When all is said and done, knowing thyself remains a simple but powerful piece of advice. Self-knowledge strengthens your immunity against bullies. Being acutely conscious of your own strengths and weaknesses bolsters your ammunition. Coupling this self-knowledge with an unshakeable self-belief and an unwavering sense of self-worth will mean you are better able to cope with any onslaught thrown you way.

Become a student of the game

Study your workplace environment and try to understand what the key stakeholders are all about. If you're in a highly competitive environment where prestige and power are at stake, it is better to be on guard. Observe what is going on. Ask questions. If you see someone being bullied and drawn into a fight with another woman, don't be too happy about being off the hook. You may be next.

Figure out the female head honcho in the company. How did she get there? What are her drivers and motivations? Do you feel anyone is overly cunning, sly or territorial?

Explore what's going at an organisational level. How do people play politics and get promoted? Who gets ahead? If women seem to be getting away with nasty or bullying behaviours, how do they do so?

If you have difficulty responding to any of these questions, it be may a sign that you haven't studied the game sufficiently. Don't think the fact you don't take part in organisational politics shields you from not being drawn into them. That's naive. Be a student of the game and stay on the front foot. (I discuss engaging in work politics in more detail in the following chapter.)

Know the signs

Are you getting some weird vibes from someone in your work group? Do you feel singled out? Do you suspect that someone might be undermining you as they act overly nice towards you? Don't take the matter lightly. All kinds of tools are available to help you get a better idea of the female psychopath/bully's modus operandi. Robert Hare's *Psychopathy Checklist*, for example, is a tool to rely on – although it should be used with caution. If you're not a trained psychologist, don't try to form a differential diagnosis or master the scoring subtleties. The value is in the questions Hare offers to check for plausibility. Take notes and record what is going on; this will help you assess if a pattern is developing or if it's just a false alarm.

As a rule, reading up on bullying will pay off – even if the information you find doesn't exactly cover your situation. You can access multiple websites and books with all kinds of examples and references to help you get the skinny on this subject. Today, when information is at the tip of your fingers, there's no need to stay in the dark.

Shake it off

Once you've noticed someone has put a target on your back, staying poised and avoiding getting riled up after first blows may be your best course of action. I'm not suggesting you let the bully step on you, but try to avoid overreacting. Bullies are attracted to those they can easily bring into their orbit. They are addicted to control, power and domination. The first blow is often a trap – a way for the bully to test the waters and see if the target will take the bait.

Don't take the bait. By responding with too much self-righteousness, you may be putting yourself at risk and exposing your vulnerability. Alternatively, ignoring and brushing it off can at times go a long way, and those tactics, while not spectacular, should not be under-estimated. You owe it to yourself to shrug it off at first and send the bully packing.

Build a shield

Learning how to build a shield is a primary tactic to dealing with bullies – although, of course, impenetrable armour doesn't exist. Being a woman at work who is driven by an eagerness to please and be liked does not put you in good stead. Coupled with wobbly self-confidence, this will make for a potentially bumpy road, especially if you have people surrounding you who test your resilience and ability to take one on the chin.

Make it your objective to boost your confidence over time. Take stock of what you bring to the table. Learn how to appreciate it and build on it.

What's the solution? Make it your objective to boost your confidence over time. Take stock of what you bring to the table. Learn how to appreciate it and build on it. Don't be dependent on the approval of others but rather try to surround yourself with a selected entourage of people you can trust. Slowly learn how to manage those who disagree with you and bring yourself to live alongside a few who may be (God forbid) disappointed with either you or your work.

As one of my clients told me recently,

The possibility of my boss being disappointed with my performance used to take up a staggering amount of my mental space! I was so consumed by it; I had forgotten that I was not exactly impressed with her management style either. This disappointment deal could work both ways! Remembering it helped me put things into perspective and muster up the courage to ask for better direction and clearer delegation. My performance improved overnight!

Consider exiting

Can you imagine knowing somebody who is scared? Say someone close to you was telling you that her boss was nuts; that she went from loving people to hating people in a heartbeat. Manipulating others was second nature to her. Mean things were going on, and things were not on the up and up. The situation couldn't be fixed by a logical or calm explanation. Your friend's boss was crazy. The environment wasn't bringing out the worst in her – her boss was using the environment to act out her mean streak. What would you tell your friend in this situation? And what would you do if you found yourself in this situation?

In these cases, the best solution may be to stay away from this person – psychopath or whatever else we may label her – as much as possible. If your boss or another colleague is acting like this, consider bringing it to HR higher-ups or any other relevant authorities to make sure at least a record is created of what is going on. You can give it your best shot and see if someone out there is up for a battle. Remember – nobody should be miserable for too long. Trying to get relocated or finding another role can be viable options. When things get too bad, however, you might not have much else to do. That's when you exit! It's a big world out there with many opportunities.

Recruit male mentors and sponsors

Engaging men in a meaningful dialogue about female aggression and bullying at work (as outlined in this chapter) cemented the profound impact that men can have if they are encouraged to actively step up as allies for gender equality and help secure the future of the next generation of female leaders.

When acting as mentors or sponsors to women at work, I advised these men never to underestimate the severity of what might be going on. They needed to be aware of the signs, offer a respectful ear, and take what they heard seriously. Seek out men who are willing to act in this way, and ask them to mentor you (formally or informally). Be brave enough to share your feelings and experiences. Ask for them to be by your side as someone you can count on.

In the next chapter, I help you figure out whether you are being targeted by a female bully – and explore in more depth what you can do about it if you are. It's so easy to sweep being bullied under the rug and rationalise the behaviour. But what if you're wrong? The next chapter can help you find out what's really going on.

Chapter 22

Are you a target?

I have experienced being blackballed, women disparaging me about my abilities and capability to do certain things. Would I call that bullying? I guess so; I am kind of on the fence about that one.

Start-Up Founder & CEO

Anyone can find themselves on the receiving end of a bully's attack. Indeed, in most cases female bullies are more likely to target other women. Still, I have found some of the ways in which women respond can mean they are more likely to become a target. Pointing out these factors is important, because unlike so many things in your work life, knowing about them and doing something about them is actually within the realm of your control. So that's what this chapter is all about.

Minimising the behaviour

The first thing that can increase your chances of becoming a bully's target is minimising their mean streak and/or believing they are worth giving multiple chances to. I have witnessed countless examples of successful leaders whose careers have come to an abrupt halt because of their belief that all people, even jerks who have proven themselves to be so, can change. Almost always, the leader is the one who ends up getting shoved out of the company and the renegade stays on, usually stepping into the leadership role pretty much unscathed.

Why does it take some of us so long to take action with employees or colleagues who behave badly? It's because most of us prefer to believe in the good of people. Am I right? Most of us want to give others the benefit of the doubt and believe in their ability to change. Most of us would also like to be thought of as kind and compassionate. But here's the truth. From a psychological perspective, after 30 years of age you're unlikely to change all that much unless you happen to go through some cataclysmic life event, such as a near-death experience, the loss of a loved one or the epiphany of finding God. I don't mean to sound cynical. I just know that to change behaviour at a fundamental level, the electrical circuitry of the brain has to literally be jump-started and re-wired for a person's behaviour to morph into an improved version of themselves.

Barring some major life-changing epiphany, your mindset and behaviours will only change if you do the work you need to do to alter your neurology. This is part of the reason growth mindset work in leadership development has gained so much traction. Trying to create a growth mindset (rather than a fixed mindset) is a way for people to work on their brains and try to outsmart their biology. This is the 'heavy lifting' of leadership work – which is also why not everyone is up for the challenge.

As a leader, not taking swift action and removing people who behave badly can result in disrespect from others and, potentially, the end of your own career with that organisation. (I have experienced this firsthand; remember Tiffany?)

As a leader, not taking swift action and removing people who behave badly can result in disrespect from others and, potentially, the end of your own career with that organisation.

At the first sniff of deceit, Jean-François and I advised Kathryn to report the conflict of interest between Emma and Preston, and cancel her involvement in the recruitment process. Kathryn felt this would be premature and wanted to wait to give Emma a go, in spite of her better judgement. In the end, Kathryn did cut off all contact with Emma, but only after a full month of Emma undermining her by spreading rumours about her incompetence and talking up Preston's alleged superiority for the role. The damage to Kathryn's reputation was difficult to quantify, but we knew for sure that her candidacy had been significantly and irreparably tainted. The scales were not balanced and Preston had the upper hand right from the get-go. In the end, Kathryn did strongarm Emma into turning herself in, but it was too little too late. She had not moved fast enough. This was a tough lesson to learn.

Kathryn had also been held back by Susan White, the first woman to make it onto the executive team at Kudos. A prominent Australian CEO I interviewed shared a similar experience to Kathryn's:

> I was only the second woman to hold the role of president. When the former president heard I was being nominated, she rang around and told people not to vote for me.

The golden rule here is if you know a colleague, staff member or client is doing things to undermine you, I act swiftly to remove them – before the situation bites you in the butt. Trust your instincts, aim and fire! The alternative is to call it quits and move on before you go down the gurgler yourself. Get out before the hurricane hits!

I don't want my advice here to sound like I am suggesting that this is a simple fix. I also want to acknowledge that not everyone is in a position to remove the bullies at work from their lives. If you're not in a position to act directly against the bully, seeking support from human resources or an employment lawyer can help you plot out a solution that will work for you. I also recommend talking to your boss about it once you've tried to solve it first – it's important that you present yourself as proactive and not defensive. However, at the end of the day, if the situation is too sticky, it may be best to remove yourself and save yourself the pain and aggravation of navigating a potential minefield that could blow up in your face.

Believing politics is only played by dickheads

I have worked with many women who simply refuse to engage in any political activity at work. They felt it was dirty, animalistic and beneath them, and did not want to go down the perceived slippery slope of being unethical. They also didn't feel they were good at it so did not see the point.

Obviously, everybody makes their own choice and has their own limits as to what they can and can't do in the name of politics. If you are aware of the consequences of staying on the sidelines, that's fine. Keep the following in mind, however: as a rule, I find women are more naturally skilled at playing politics while staying true to their values. They are able to manage their impact, get support for their decisions and act with a conscience.

This ability all comes from building genuine relationships – starting with the people you like and with whom connecting requires minimal effort. In coaching terms, when discussing the quality of key strategic relationships, I refer to the level of energy required to build or maintain the connection as the 'level of nurture'. This term is not new and is commonly used among sales professionals. I ask my clients, 'What is the level of nurture required in this relationship? Is it low, medium or high?' The response dictates the amount of energy required to improve or maintain the relationship.

In our journey with Kathryn, Jean-François and I found that Kathryn chose to spend too much time with her head down, making sure she was focused on the daily grind, meeting deadlines and producing great-quality work. This is such a common mistake. She would have been better served spending more time on understanding the motivations and behaviours of others. This would have enhanced the quality of her relationships with significant players in her organisation.

Being better connected would have paved the way for a much fairer match.

Not finding your authentic voice

Another challenge is to find your confident and assertive voice – and many women struggle with this one. Too often, they go from a quiet and understanding stance to being overly pushy and hell-bent on telling it like it is. They struggle to find the middle ground – or, to put it in different terms, they take a while to fine-tune the right voice.

Being able to find your authentic voice – one that commands respect and inspires confidence – is a key strategy to keep bullies at bay. For Kathryn, finding this voice was especially challenging. For years, she tended to dilute the power of her communication by prefacing what she was saying with phrases such as, 'I'm sorry', 'Could you do me a favour', and 'I was wondering if there was any way you could'. The first visible step in Kathryn's shift required her to be conscious of these phrases and actively change the way she spoke to get things done. This meant resisting the urge to pad her dialogue and learning to become more direct and straightforward.

> *Being able to find your authentic voice – one that commands respect and inspires confidence – is a key strategy to keep bullies at bay.*

Kathryn tried, but like so many other women, her shift from doormat to badass was quite dramatic. Fuelled partly by her ambitions and partly by the repressed anger she had been feeling over the years because of putting her own needs on the back burner, she went all out. She suddenly told the truth! My job as a coach is to speak the truth and help others speak theirs. This doesn't mean, however, that a leader should always say what they are really thinking no matter what.

Too much truth can lead to your demise, and fast. Deep down, most people can't handle the truth told to them too bluntly. They don't want to hear bad news and are unprepared to deal with the brutal facts, or to look in the mirror – particularly if that truth is about them.

As Charles de Gaulle (leader of the Free French Forces against Nazi Germany in World War II and president of France from 1959 to 1969) once said, 'The great leaders have always stage-managed their effects'. Successful leadership requires the leader to be an organisational politician, skilled in the art of transforming into a chameleon and changing skin when required. I'm not suggesting that leaders become liars. But what I am proposing is careful planning around how to present a view that may be taboo or contrary to popular perception. It needs to be done skilfully and gracefully to be digestible. So be authentic yes, but not too much.

At some point in her journey, Kathryn got fed up and decided to hit them all between the eyes, raising all the contentious truths she could muster. I respected Kathryn's 'big balls' attitude but feared that behind the clapping and smiles it provoked more shock than admiration. In hindsight, her change was too drastic and thus ill-advised.

To her credit, she was smart enough to recognise the need for balance and, in time, made significant improvements. Developing her own memorable and unique voice was a key factor in preparing herself for high-level office politics, which led to her success.

Wasting your seven seconds

Research shows we all have about seven seconds to make a good impression. If I had a dollar for how many times I've spoken to my clients about being well groomed, making the most of all their physical assets, having good manners and dressing to impress to be more successful, I'd own my paradise island by now. Wearing a fabulous smile is also priceless.

What's interesting is the reaction I often get. Many of my clients – and especially women – look at me as if I am either full of it, or deeply superficial. Note that I'm not replicating here the kind of advice Ernst & Young issued to their female employees, where they were advised to 'dress fit and not provocatively' (which I mention in chapter 18). However, the bottom line is this is serious business – so much so that professionals such as Diane Craig, a very well-networked image and etiquette consultant from Ottawa in Canada, makes a great living from helping politicians and international dignitaries overhaul their image to get more votes and increase their likeability quotient (or LQ). Yes, a profession exists that provides a service like this. Likeability quotient is defined as the 'level of happiness and wellbeing that you arise in others'.[85] In the same way, the reverse is true. The more unpleasant others find you, the more difficulties you are likely to encounter in life and at work. Honest.

This can become particularly difficult when dealing with psychopaths, because they can really tune in to your needs and what you find acceptable. They then use this information to manipulate you into giving them what they want. They are experts at impression management, making sure that they present the exact image that you want to see. Likewise, narcissists believe that they are a gift to the planet and will make sure that others know how good they are. This impression management will see them showcase their best attributes while downplaying or even lying about those of others.

So, as much of a cad as Preston Steele was, he knew the benefits of having a well-managed image and did what he had to do to maintain a high LQ. He was naturally a happy and passionate guy. People left conversations with him feeling motivated, energised and on a high. His smile alone left others bedazzled. Kathryn was equally passionate, but far more serious in nature. People respected Kathryn's intellect; however, they did not usually invite her out for drinks. For women presenting with a double whammy of warmth and competence is what gets them asked back for another round. This is a psychological fact. It enhances their influence and maximises their impact at work.[86]

Preston made himself well liked by noticing the details about people and really listening. You've likely heard the expression, 'it's the little things that make a difference'. Preston, like so many others, had this down pat. When he decided it mattered, he remembered people's birthdays and the names of their spouses and partners, and had a great memory for recalling people's hobbies and interests. This meant most people felt valued after talking to Preston. Because he remembered the minutiae about their lives, they felt as if he had really listened.

As with most things related to Preston, this was all a trick. On one of the few occasions he interacted with me, he showed me the technique he used to remember things. When he made a new contact, he'd write down a few things he'd learned about them on the back on their business card (for example, 'George: divorced, rides a Harley, likes Coldplay'). That way, if he ever had to connect with that person again, he had something to talk about. He had a great conversation starter, and people were always super impressed he'd remembered some small detail about them. I also heard a rumour from others who knew him well that he used to boast about his technique being a 'leg opener'. Pretty crass, but you've still got to hand it to him. It was a clever strategy on all fronts.

Preston's rugged good looks didn't hurt him either. Sex sells and Preston used his physical assets to full advantage. He looked like he could already be a chief executive officer with his well-styled locks and perfectly pressed suits, and research into upping your LQ shows an exponential rise occurs when attractiveness is added to the mix. Kathryn was an equally stunning woman; however, she tended to downplay her 'assets', so her good looks were not a focus. She wanted to be taken seriously. We're not sure whether this helped or hindered her. Being a good-looking woman does not always work to your advantage with other women, but it likely wouldn't have hurt her popularity with the male contingent.

I'm going to dare ask you the question – are you making the most of what you have to offer?

At the end of the day, despite Preston's unscrupulous tactics for getting in the door at Kudos, a lot remains to be learned about getting ahead from the powerful tactics he utilised to leverage himself at Kudos and become a formidable contender for the top job.

I'm going to dare ask you the question – are you making the most of what you have to offer?

In the next chapter, I explore in more detail some of the ingrained behaviours and social conditioning that might be holding you back from stepping into your potential and having the career and life you want.

Chapter 23

Stop being so bloody nice

It takes a great deal of bravery to stand up to our enemies, but just as much to stand up to our friends.

Dumbledore in J.K. Rowling's
Harry Potter and the Philosopher's Stone

Being stabbed in the back, treated poorly and bullied is painful. It hurts us deeply because it harms, violates, damages and confounds us at the deepest parts of ourselves. It attacks our self-worth.

Jean-François and I have stood alongside and supported count-less clients going through the pain and torment of being mistreated, abused and bullied during our careers as psychologists. A large part of the inspiration for this book was a beautiful woman we worked with who ended up taking her own life in reaction to years of being bullied by another female executive on her team. Crystal, like many women at the executive table, believed she had to be as tough as nails, act like a man and not share her emotions to be taken seriously. She suffered in silence for years while her pride and self-respect took such a beating that it broke her spirit. Like Kathryn, she had driven to her lake house for some welcome respite. The only difference was she went for a midnight swim and never came back.

Being at the top is hard enough already, and for women even more so. I remember the enlightening insight that David, the former CEO of a food manufacturing company, shared with me about his life at the helm. His words helped me to take on his emotional perspective and recognise how isolated and lonely it feels to be an executive, let alone adding a bullying experience in the mix.

David told me:

You know, I can't really talk to anyone. When you get into this job, if you share your weaknesses, fears and emotions you are seen as incompetent and not fit to run the company. So obviously I can't talk to the board about this. I can't talk to my peers because they are in competition with me and will use stuff I say to their advantage. I can't talk to my direct reports because they'll just lose respect for me and see me a useless leader who they wouldn't like to follow. That's why I hired you; you are my safe place.

Seeing a beautiful soul like Crystal psychologically unravel was tantamount to watching a slow death. For Crystal, and many people who are bullied, the personalised nature of bullying is what destabilises and disassembles their identity and ego bit by bit. What follows are excessive feelings of frustration and an overwhelming sense of injustice, helplessness and profound sadness for almost anyone who has gone through it.

No more suffering in silence

This begs the question: why do people stay silent about an invisible epidemic so destructive that it is taking lives along with it?

Why didn't Crystal ask for help or make a stand to fight against what was happening to her? Because she rationalised it instead, blamed herself and made excuses. Like most type-A 'Wonder Woman' sorts, she felt like she should be able to handle it and explain it away.

'I'm probably over-sensitive', she told us. 'It's just a personality difference, a style issue; I'm taking things too personally.'

Having mixed feelings is normal when you're the target of bullying – including guilt for having given so much control to the bully, and then shame and humiliation for not having done enough to put an end to it.

Having mixed feelings is normal when you're the target of bullying – including guilt for having given so much control to the bully, and then shame and humiliation for not having done enough to put an end to it. One thing is certain: the longer the exposure to the stressor, the more severe the psychological impact will be. Psychosomatic symptoms such as anxiety, panic attacks, depression and post-traumatic stress usually follow (reams of anecdotal evidence confirm this).

When all is said and done, the sad reality is that it takes a person feeling unwell and a seeing a doctor before the real impact of bullying is finally discovered. Going through a potential ordeal all alone, however, is pointless. Get out of the arena before the attacks get worse, and save yourself. Sometimes, simply taking the time to put your ideas together and discuss them with a trusted advisor helps put things in perspective. Talking and sharing often helps. You are not alone and there is no shame in expressing honestly what you are experiencing. Plus, experts are available. Why not benefit from their experience?

Let's hear from a client who sought help after suffering in silence for far too long:

> I spent months alone ruminating ... struggling to decide if I was being a drama queen or if there was really something to be worried about. Months! After I shared my situation with my ex-mentor, he laid down the law and helped me figure out a game plan in a 30-minute conversation. I felt like a fool – a relieved fool – but a fool nonetheless for having waited so long.

Don't wait until you're too far gone to seek help.

The quiet achiever rarely wins the race

Women are socialised to play nice. From the time we're born, we're forced into the mould of caregiver and nurturer to prepare us for our potential future roles as wives and mothers. Once we hit the working world, it's no different. Most women continue to respect our traditionally ascribed roles, play by the social rules, and feel that being thought of as mean is akin to having rabies.

In this context, it is easy to see how the early signs of being abused and/or bullied can be minimised or tossed aside. Women are not ready for a fight. Worst yet, they tend to project on others this aura of niceness they have integrated. In other words, they expect others to be like them: nice and well meaning. When it turns out somebody is not, they are unprepared and caught off guard.

In our leadership story from part I, Kathryn behaved as you would expect any 'good woman' to behave before her move to become CEO of Kudos. She was accommodating and gracious. She often put others first at her own expense. Feeling needed and playing the sacrificial lamb made her feel good. It met her need to feel like a good person, a person that people would like.

Without doubt, her great interpersonal skills and natural way of engaging also helped her forge a successful career at Kudos. Her political savvy didn't hurt her career either. Kathryn raised her political capital in the organisation by engaging in generous acts of service. She ingratiated herself by being nice, low maintenance and easy to get along with, and her caring, service-oriented style won friends and helped her to influence people to get ahead.

However, the reality is what got Kathryn the vice-president's role wouldn't get her into the CEO's chair. Kathryn was not viewed as the natural successor to the CEO, despite her impressive track record and high likability quotient.[87]

This is because being nice and caring is not associated with strength. It is seen as weak and soft. Her tendency to be overly consultative to appear collaborative did not help her cause either. It just made her appear indecisive. As is the case for so many other women, I knew if Kathryn was to have any chance of making it to the top, she needed to shake off her 'Mary Poppins' image and be seen as tougher and able to stand alone in her decision-making. Putting focus on building a stronger base of allies both inside and outside Kudos to increase her personal brand and market value was also a key strategy for success. To be seen as the future CEO of Kudos, Kathryn had to

exude strength – without being seen as aggressive or as trying to be one of the guys at work.

Women are known to have a really hard time doing that because they are socialised to put everyone else first – something known (in Australia and New Zealand at least) as the 'burnt chop syndrome'.

Just stay with me on this.

Picture this: a mother is preparing the evening meal for her family. She has bought the juiciest, most succulent lamb chops and is searing them on the grill. (Apologies to any vegetarian or vegan friends – this is for illustration purposes only.) The smell is intoxicating, and she can't wait to tuck in. Cooking them at the same time as all the other responsibilities and distractions in her life, most of them come out beautifully – except one of them gets a little too charred. Who gets served up that inferior chop at dinner time? She does, putting it on her plate as punishment for her sins and because everyone else deserves the better options. It's her fault after all.

Whether you are a mother or not, you get the gist. And the metaphor doesn't relate to just food, either. Women (and girls) will often allow others to have what they want, and make do with what is left. Being able to create a world where men and women are treated equally starts at home.

Making the shift from nice girl to badass

Making the shift from nice girl to badass is totally doable but first you have to wrestle with some big faulty assumptions.

A plethora of evidence demonstrates that as effective as some leaders may be, success is not guaranteed as a result. This is where many effective leaders like Kathryn miss the mark. She assumed that the mere fact of doing a good job and her staff liking her warranted a promotion and more likely paved the way for a step up. Interestingly, this widely held urban myth is rife in the corporate world, where the notion of the quiet achiever eventually becoming a powerful leader provides an excuse for many, particularly the more introverted, to fly under the radar and hide in their cubicles. The result is usually that they remain where they have placed themselves, unknown and under a rock – in some cases, gathering moss.

Shying away from being seen is foolish. Organisational landscapes are inherently political arenas so committing to actively building your profile and managing it is a non-negotiable if you want to get ahead. This is because traditional decision-making models don't usually reflect the principles of fairness, rationality and professionalism, but rather reflect the informal power struggles designed to protect or enhance the self-interest of conflicting individuals or groups in a hierarchical system. This system is what opened the door for slime bags like Preston to be more successful at climbing the leadership ladder than Kathryn. Despite her impressive track record and great interpersonal skills, she was unwilling to jump into the political ring. Preston was a fierce competitor because he knew the stakes were high and was proactive about playing the game.

So many men and women I have coached over the years have expressed their distaste for promoting themselves and getting noticed – particularly in Australia where the 'tall poppy syndrome' reigns supreme. (An example here is Kylie Minogue, the international pop star also affectionately but somewhat derogatorily known as the 'singing budgie' who fled to England because of the all the grief she had to put up with from haters in Australia – only to be welcomed back decades later after she had 'made it'.)

Without question, Kathryn's reluctance to raise her profile, coupled with her lack of desire to convert any potential saboteurs into raving fans, meant that she shot herself in the foot. Jean-François and I were hoping it wasn't too late for her to step up.

Toughening up and becoming a badass overnight can be difficult. You don't want to become someone you feel is not consistent with you true authentic self. So what can you do? Here's my advice:

- *Draw the line*: If you're worried about being seen as disingenuous, make a clear distinction between your work persona and your family/friend persona. This means shining up your battle armour at work and remaining nice to your friends after hours – one does not exclude the other.

- *Leverage your strengths:* Focus on tapping into your strongest personality traits or idiosyncrasies, and then leverage them fully. This is a real skill, and a wonderful example of this is my client Suzie. She had the 'gift of the gab' and knew how to put forward powerful arguments. When she received feedback to tone it down, her response was to go silent instead for fear of being seen as overbearing. I coached her to do the opposite – to raise the volume and strive to make verbal communication a compelling differentiator for her at work to be heard and seen. In time, Suzie became known for her ability to stand her ground and call out people's mean-spirited attacks right off the bat. She might not have become the ultimate warrior, but she knew enough to defend herself and use her voice as a weapon for positive change.

Proactive and graceful self-promotion is a sophisticated and essential leadership skill, particularly for women.

The lesson here for anyone with powerful leadership aspirations who resists the urge to get noticed because they believe actions speak for themselves is that it's probably time to jump into the discomfort and leap onto the radar. Proactive and graceful self-promotion is a sophisticated and essential leadership skill, particularly for women.

In the next chapter, I move into providing a vision of what's possible, and an alternative we all could strive for.

Chapter 24

Let's bake a new pie

It's not about a piece of the existing pie; there are too many of us for that. It's about baking a new pie.

Gloria Steinem

The aim of this book is to let the truth out.

Even amid the risk of disagreement or disapproval from other women, this is a conversation that has been driven by (in Catherine Fox's terms) 'righteous fury'[88] and using my frustration instead of suppressing it 'to get things done'.

Think about Julia Gillard's famous misogyny speech to parliament in 2012. Her words reverberated around the world and the speech became a pivotal moment for all women everywhere. She dared to say what no-one else would – that the then leader of the opposition, Tony Abbott, had 'repulsive double standards when it comes to misogyny and sexism', and that he 'should think seriously about the role of women in public life'.

So here it is. Here's my truth.

Men aren't the only ones strengthening the glass ceiling and pushing women over the glass cliff. The way some women treat each other at work has created an additional barrier to women getting ahead – the sisterhood ceiling. The problem is that by opposing the attempts of other females to advance in their careers, some women are perpetuating the cultural stigmas already held against women in the workplace.

If we listen to the researchers, we may argue that women have no control over being nasty, that women cannot make conscious choices. The reality is we all discriminate unconsciously – no-one is guilt free. Unconscious discrimination is defined as the act of unknowingly discriminating against someone. Whether you choose to believe it or not, we all do it and our biases influence not only our worldview but also our decision-making, sometimes without us even knowing. That's the scary part.

Suggesting we can eliminate unconscious biases forever is unrealistic. However, being more aware of them may enable us to limit their impact on how we behave and so lead to more mindful choices. Whether you have had a direct experience or not, women may engage in bullying behaviours without fully realising the impact, because these tactics have become normalised in certain cultures, environments and workplaces. Becoming more well informed about how we are responding to our workplace cultures can only increase our self-awareness, so that deciding whether to be nasty or not becomes a conscious choice.

Becoming more well informed about how we are responding to our workplace cultures can only increase our self-awareness, so that deciding whether to be nasty or not becomes a conscious choice.

You are not justified to bully someone because you've been bullied before. Just because you feel that's the way it goes in your organisation (or at school), doesn't make it right. You can't justify being a bully by saying you can't help it or by calling it tough love. Think twice. Acknowledge your inner mean streak and fight off your instinct to be a jerk. Another way is always possible. You owe it to everybody to find it and improve.

I spoke about the behaviour of chimpanzees, the socio-species closest to humans, in chapter 18. Let's return to our great apes to find substantiation for the possibility of alternative behaviour. Another member of the great ape family is the bonobo – also the closest relative to humans. Bonobo society has a dominant matriarchal culture where certain females are higher in social standing than males and govern the tribe. (While every community is dominated by a female, some males will still obtain a high rank in the hierarchy.) Described as 'peace-loving primates',[89] primatologist Frans de Waal stated bonobos were indeed capable of altruism, compassion, empathy, kindness, patience and sensitivity. He described bonobo society as a 'gynecocracy', meaning 'women's government over women and men' or 'women's social supremacy.' Interestingly, researchers of bonobos have found minimal aggression takes place between the sexes and that conflict is usually resolved by 'making love and not war'.

What is clear to me is that the key to creating a world where women are treated as equals rests in the hands of all of us. Women also need to commit to being more aware of the biological drives and unconscious biases and behaviours that inadvertently block and punish members of the sisterhood at work – and work towards eliminating them.

Seeking opportunities to work together is a sure-fire way to increase female representation at the top and decrease the need to play dirty politics to get ahead. A woman-against-woman career strategy will not get us any closer to having the career we dream about.

> *Seeking opportunities to work together is a sure-fire way to increase female representation at the top and decrease the need to play dirty politics to get ahead.*

After 20 years of working with women and men, I've seen firsthand the imitable magic that happens when women come together, giving each other the space to show up as their authentic selves, being able to safely voice their blockers and leave strengthened with clarity and resolve to lead their way and chase their greatest ambitions.

Reflecting on the bonobos, I cannot help but wonder how different things would be if we were more focused on making peace and not war. What could be achieved if women of the world were truly united and focused on working together with men to build a community of equals?

One thing I know for sure is that not supporting each other is one of the greatest threats to all of us having the life we want, and it's going to take all of us to make it happen.

Standing in front of a room of illustrious women at Davos, I was humbled by the desire for building the sisterhood and the acknowledgement that working together better will increase gender parity. Julia Dudenko, global council member for the Global Council for Responsible AI and Group CSIO at Haniel, a German company overseeing the cybersecurity strategy for major corporations globally, said this:

> During the intensive days of WEF25 in Davos, a powerful theme emerged: the sisterhood of female leaders. It was about understanding, supporting, and empowering one another. The event showcased inspiring examples of women leading with entrepreneurship, foresight, innovation, and compassion ... The sisterhood I experienced at WEF25 was both inspiring and transformative. Together, we can continue breaking barriers, lifting each other up, and creating a world where female leadership knows no borders and drives meaningful change ... The future is HUMAN, it embodies EQUALITY, and we laid the foundation at WEF25.

I think we are more ready than we have ever been to listen, to hear and create the positive turbulence we need to create the change we want to see.

In the next chapter, I outline a multipronged approach to help you start strategising how to achieve a noteworthy upward swing of the pendulum and shift the dial once and for all.

Chapter 25

Stop talking and start walking

When life's hills become too steep to climb on my own, my sister takes my hand and reminds me that I didn't have to climb it alone to begin with.

Unknown

By now you would have figured it out. No silver bullet exists to achieve gender parity. We need to do the work – transformation is an inside job and it starts with us.

To equip you for the trek that lies ahead, this fully revised and updated edition comes jam-packed with psychological tools, techniques and strategies to help you navigate the complex and muddy dynamics of female hostility and bullying at work. And if change is to be supported, a multi-pronged review of the systems we need to build is required to reinforce and sustain long-awaited momentum.

Based on my research, and the wisdom and experience gained in the trenches, here are some ideas that bring together individual strategies, organisational policies and broader societal shifts to address the complex roots of this issue:

- *Raise awareness and education:* Training and exploration of likely scenarios is needed to help people recognise and understand the different types of bullying behaviours. As part of this training, encouraging open discussions and reflections on personal experiences and biases is critical. This helps make it meaningful for participants and creates commitment to change.
- *Promote self-awareness and accountability:* Women should be encouraged to reflect on their own behaviours and the potential impact on others. This will help to foster a culture where women are willing to call out problematic behaviours, even in themselves.
- *Build supportive networks and partnerships:* Women need to be supported to find 'tribes' and personal boards of advisors, both male and female, to provide guidance and support. Establishing formal mentorship programs to connect younger women with more experienced leaders works well too. (I am a proud mentor for emerging

female leaders with WIMWA – Women in Mining WA. They have created something magical and provide this guidance and support well.)

- *Review organisational policies and leadership*: Implementing clear anti-bullying policies and procedures within organisations is paramount. Encouraging male leaders to also take an active role in supporting and advocating for women will cement adherence to these policies. Ensuring HR and leadership teams are responsive to reports of bullying, rather than dismissing the claims or protecting the perpetrators, will provide further reinforcement.
- *Encourage intergenerational dialogue and understanding*: One area I haven't touched on in depth is the need to facilitate discussions between the younger and older generations of women to bridge the gap in expectations and experiences. Helping younger women understand the challenges faced by previous generations, and how they might have shaped existing trends and behaviours, is important to create the change we want to see early on.
- *Shift the narrative on societal expectations*: Challenging the assumption that all women should automatically support and 'lift' up other women is an important discussion, because this assumption can create unrealistic demands. Instead, promoting a more balanced view of women's roles and responsibilities in the workplace might be a more constructive place to reframe expectations of what a woman 'should be' and how much they 'should' give.

In the final chapter, I leave you with my dream for the future. I hope it inspires you and compels you to be part of the change.

Chapter 26

Creating a new tomorrow

Stand before the people you fear and speak your mind – even if your voice shakes.

Maggie Kuhn

I'd like to leave you with some final thoughts. Writing this book has been a triggering experience. Partly because of the polarity that exists in the sisterhood about the existence of this phenomenon, I was worried about how this book might be received. Partly, this was because of my own personal experiences with female aggression – first as a little girl at school (I come from a non-English-speaking background and so had a bit of an accent, which made me a target) and then later as a leader in the working world (becoming an executive early in my career didn't win many female friends at the time).

However, the urge to write this piece was stronger than my fears. I was compelled to put this out into the world, and the book wrote itself as my fingers flew off the keyboard, directing me with every tap.

I kept thinking about it like this: *what is that one thing I would shout from the top of the tallest mountain for the world to hear if I weren't afraid of the repercussions?*

And this is often the dilemma of speaking up – pushing past the fear and doing it anyway. I knew that releasing this new edition meant putting myself out of my comfort zone to become a target through leading a vital conversation – all the while nervous to be viewed as a traitor by my 'sisters'. But I feared doing nothing, and that choosing inactivity over proactive action would widen the gender gap and contribute more to the problem we are still battling.

Creating a new tomorrow starts with us. The shrinkage of gender parity is a reminder that even one woman matters to the equation.

In preparing to re-release this book, I spoke to a colleague I deeply respected about what we needed to do to really get gender equality right. She talked to me about the need to 'whisper' to get a guernsey at the game.

Well, I don't think that's working out that well for us in Australia.

Creating a new tomorrow starts with us. The shrinkage of gender parity is a reminder that even one woman matters to the equation. I think it's time to stop whispering, don't you?

I am calling on you, dear reader, to dream bigger and to find purpose in solving one of the most complex social challenges we are facing as women.

We don't have a pipeline issue.[90] Women who aspire to power evoke far more resistance from deeply rooted barriers, some of which have been surfaced in this book.

It's time to turn our whispers into sweeter sounding roars. Imagine if we all committed to raising one woman up per year – how that would change things for the better?

But solving these issues does start with looking more deeply into what is causing the gender imbalance, and being brave enough to take responsibility for the part we might be playing in it, before it's too late.

It's time to turn our whispers into sweeter sounding roars. Imagine if we all committed to raising one woman up per year – how would that change things for the better? It doesn't take much but it will take all of us.

I'd like to leave you with this call to action:

Find out what ignites worlds within you. Now, more than ever, the world needs more light.

Discover what sparks your world and find the people who whole-heartedly believe in it.

Use this spark to go and change something. Even if your voice shakes.

This is your world. Go and shape it or someone else will.

I'd love to hear from you about your reactions to this book, and your experiences – either with female bullying or your own efforts to shape your world and lift other women. You can contact me via the following:

- vanessa@vanessavershaw.com
- www.linkedin.com/in/vanessa-vershaw/
- www.instagram.com/vanessavershaw/
- www.facebook.com/VanessaVershaw

About the author

An elite high-performance workplace psychologist, entrepreneur and transformation strategist, Vanessa Vershaw is a trusted advisor to executives and key decision-makers of ASX-20 and Fortune 100 companies globally.

Using a potent combination of psychology, design thinking, neuroscience and ancient wisdom, Vanessa helps leaders from around the world reimagine their futures, sparking bold thinking and solving extreme challenges in the areas of strategy, culture, workforce development, organisational resilience, innovation and creativity.

A champion for social justice and gender equality, Vanessa won the Momentum Trailblazer of the Year award for her work empowering women to reach for the stars and create the life and careers they dream about. This led to her representing APAC and speaking at the 2025 World Woman Foundation in Davos, Switzerland. She is also the award-winning author of *Unreasonable Ambition: Renegade Thinking for Leaders to Create Impossible Change*.

Endnotes

1   The World Economic Forum at Davos is an annual meeting for over 3000 world leaders, business heads and top experts from more than 125 countries. These people come together to address topics on a variety of issues – from global cooperation to the climate crisis affecting people and the planet, and, of course, diversity, equity and inclusion.

2   Duke, S (2023). 'Economic shocks are wiping out progress on gender equality: Global Gender Gap Report 2023', World Economic Forum. Available: weforum.org/stories/2023/06/economics-shocks-gender-equality-linkedin/; see also Fox, C (2024). *Breaking the Boss Bias: How to Get More Women into Leadership*. New South Books. Sydney, NSW.

3   Fox, C (2022). 'The trap of over-optimism'. catherinefox.com.au. Available: catherinefox.com.au/the-trap-of-over-optimism/.

4   Plan International (2023). *Gender Compass: A Segmentation of Australia's Views on Gender Equality*. Available: plan.org.au/wp-content/uploads/2023/09/GenderCompass_Report.pdf

5   See, for example, Smith, JL, McPartlan, P, Poe, J & Thoman, DB (2021). 'Diversity fatigue: A survey for measuring attitudes towards diversity enhancing efforts in academia'. *Cultural Diversity and Ethnic Minority Psychology*, 27(4), 659–674. doi.org/10.1037/cdp0000406.

6   See, for example, Patten, S (2024). 'Why the backlash from men is threatening gender targets'. *Financial Review*. 28 November.

7   Megan McCracken is the 2021 winner of the Industry Advocate category of the National Women in Industry Awards.

8   Patten, S (2024). 'Why the backlash from men is threatening gender targets'. *Financial Review*. 28 November.

9   To access the full report from CEW, along with the reports from 2022 and 2023, go to cew.org.au/research-resources/research.

10   According the 2024 Workplace Bullying Institute's *U.S. Workplace Bullying Survey*, 18 per cent of 'worst case situations' of bullying at work were women targeting women. See Namie, G (2024). *2024 WBI U.S. Workplace Bullying Survey*. Workplace Bullying Institute. Available: workplacebullying.org/wp-content/uploads/2024/10/2024-Complete-Report.pdf.

11   For more on this tactic, see Shallcross, L, Ramsay, S & Barker, M (2013). 'Severe workplace conflict: The experience of mobbing'. *Negotiation and Conflict Management Research*, 6(3), 191–213.

12   According to Collins Dictionary, trolling someone is when you 'deliberately try to upset them or start an argument with them, especially by posting offensive or unkind things on the internet'; see also eSafety Commissioner (n.d.). 'Trolling'. Available: esafety.gov.au/young-people/trolling.

13   For more information, see Australian Human Rights Commission (n.d.). 'Cyberbullying'. Available: humanrights.gov.au/our-work/commission-general/cyberbullying.

14   De Bortoli, L, Underwood, C, Friedman, T & Gebhardt, E (2022). *PISA 2022 Reporting Australia's results, Volume II: Student and school characteristics*. Australian Council for Educational Research. Available: research.acer.edu.au/cgi/viewcontent.cgi?article=1058&context=ozpisa.

15   Mental Health UK (2024). *The Burnout Report 2024*. Mental Health UK. Available: euc7zxtct58.exactdn.com/wp-content/uploads/2024/01/19145241/Mental-Health-UK_The-Burnout-Report-2024.pdf.

16   Ballard, A & Bozin, D (2023). 'The true financial costs of workplace violence in Australia'. *Alternative Law Journal*, 48 (3).

17 Fox, C (2024). *Breaking the Boss Bias: How to Get More Women into Leadership*. New South Books. Sydney, NSW.

18 Kurter, H (2020). 'Women bullied at work: Here's why your female boss doesn't support you'. *Forbes*. Available: forbes.com/sites/heidilynnekurter/2020/02/19/women-bullied-at-work-heres-why-your-female-boss-dislikes-you/.

19 Namie, G (2021). 'Gender of Perpetrators and Targets'. *2024 WBI U.S. Workplace Bullying Survey*. Workplace Bullying Institute. Available: workplacebullying.org/wp-content/uploads/2024/10/2024-Complete-Report.pdf.

20 World Risk Poll. (n.d.). *Digging Deeper: Global Experiences of Workplace Violence and Harassment*. World Risk Poll. Available: wrp.lrfoundation.org.uk/news/digging-deeper-global-experiences-of-workplace-violence-and-harassment#:~:text=For%20example%2C%20Australia%20and%20New,reported%20workplace%20violence%20and%20harassment.

21 McCracken, M (2017). 'Kalannie Speech for Brookfield Rail 2017' (Unpublished).

22 Rumbens, D (2022). *Breaking the Norm: Unleashing Australia's Economic Potential*. Deloitte. Available: deloitte.com/au/en/services/financial-advisory/blogs/breaking-the-norm-unleashing-australias-economic-potential.html.

23 Between 2015 and 2024, I conducted interviews with 55 male leaders in Australia, Canada and Indonesia. In 2024, I delved deeper through face-to-face interviews with five male leaders and 14 female, along with discussions with 11 women as part of a research roundtable.

24 See, for example, Nandkeolyar, AK, Bagger, J & Ekkirala, S (2022). 'Damned if she does, damned if she doesn't: The interactive effects of gender and agreeableness on performance evaluation'. *Journal of Business Research*, 143, 62–71. doi.org/10.1016/j.jbusres.2022.01.066.

25 Homayuni, A, Hosseini, Z, Aghamolaei, T & Shahini, S (2021). 'Which nurses are victims of bullying: The role of negative affect,

core self-evaluations, role conflict and bullying in the nursing staff'. *BMC Nursing*, 20(1), 57–57. doi.org/10.1186/s12912-021-00578-3.

26 Namie. G (2024). *2024 WBI U.S. Workplace Bullying Survey.* Workplace Bullying Institute. Available: workplacebullying.org/wp-content/uploads/2024/10/2024-Complete-Report.pdf

27 Ballard, A & Bozin, D (2023). 'The true (financial) costs of workplace violence in Australia'. *Alternative Law Journal*, 48(3), 191–196. doi.org/10.1177/1037969X231174672.

28 Green, A & Hart, CM (2024). 'Mean girls in disguise? Associations between vulnerable narcissism and perpetration of bullying among women'. *Sex Roles*, 90(7), 848–858. doi: 10.1007/s11199-024-01477-y

29 Safe Work Australia. (2021). *Psychosocial Health and Safety and Bullying in Australia Workplaces: Indicators from Accepted Workers' Compensation Claims.* Safe Work Australia. Available: safeworkaustralia.gov.au/sites/default/files/2021-06/D21%20 9238%20Psychosocial_health_and_safety_and_bullying_in_ australian_workplaces_6th_edition.pdf.

30 Australian Government (n.d.). 'Women in leadership'. Workplace Gender Equality Agency. Available: wgea.gov.au/women-in-leadership.

31 IESE Business School of University of Navarra (2018). 'The best places to be a woman: Countries that prioritize female leadership'. IESE Insight. Available: iese.edu/insight/articles/women-leadership-index-countries/#:~:text=The%20countries%20that%20rank%20 highest%20for%20social%20leadership,in%20the%20index%20 with%20no%20paid%20maternity%20leave.

32 Australian Government (n.d.). 'Women in leadership'. Workplace Gender Equality Agency. Available: wgea.gov.au/women-in-leadership.

33 United Nations (n.d.) 'International Equal Pay Day, 18 September: Equal pay for work of equal value'. United Nations. Available un.org/en/observances/equal-pay-day.

34　Australian Government (2024). 'Status of Women Report Card 2024'. Australian Government. Available: genderequality.gov.au/status-women-report-cards/2024-report-card.

35　Bryant, A (2013). 'Four executives on succeeding in business as a woman'. *The New York Times*. Available: nytimes.com/newsgraphics/2013/10/13/ipad/women-corner-office.html.

36　Akhtar, A (2019). 'An EY seminar reportedly suggested women have small brains'. *Financial Review*. Available: afr.com/companies/professional-services/an-ernst-and-young-seminar-reportedly-suggested-women-have-small-brains-20191025-p53446.

37　Criado Perez, C (2019). *Invisible Women: Exposing Data Bias in a World Designed for Men*. Vintage, UK.

38　Nandkeolyar, AK, Bagger, J & Ekkirala, S (2022). 'Damned if she does, damned if she doesn't: The interactive effects of gender and agreeableness on performance evaluation'. *Journal of Business Research*, 143, 62–71. doi.org/10.1016/j.jbusres.2022.01.066.

39　Hall, LJ & Donaghue, N (2013). '"Nice girls don't carry knives": Constructions of ambition in media coverage of Australia's first female prime minister'. *British Journal of Social Psychology*, 52(4), 631–647. doi.org/10.1111/j.2044-8309.2012.02114.x.

40　Roe, I (2024). 'Coalition MP says women in child care "not the same" as men in construction during gender pay debate'. *ABC News*. Available: amp-abc-net-au.cdn.ampproject.org/c/s/amp.abc.net.au/article/104673400.

41　See, for example, Spence Laschinger, HK, Wong, CA & Grau, AL (2012). 'The influence of authentic leadership on newly graduated nurses' experiences of workplace bullying, burnout and retention outcomes: A cross-sectional study'. *International Journal of Nursing Studies*, 49(10), 1266–1276. doi.org/10.1016/j.ijnurstu.2012.05.012; Beauregard, N, Marchand, A, Bilodeau, J, Durand, P, Demers, A & Haines, VY (2018). 'Gendered pathways to burnout: Results from the SALVEO study'. *Annals of Work Exposures and Health*, 62(4), 426–437, doi.org/10.1093/annweh/wxx114; Cox, J (2021), 'Why women are

more burned out than men'. BBC. Available: bbc.com/worklife/
article/20210928-why-women-are-more-burned-out-than-men.

42 Witherspoon, R (n.d.). 'If you want to change the stories, you
    need to change the storytellers'. Hellosunshine. Available: hello-
    sunshine.com/about-us/.

43 Caliper Research & Development Department (2014). *Women
    Leaders Research Paper*. Caliper. Available: calipermedia.calipercorp.
    com.s3.amazonaws.com/whitepapers/us/Women-Leaders-2014.pdf.

44 Arnocky, S, Davis, AC & Vaillancourt, T (2023). 'Resource scarcity
    predicts women's intrasexual competition: The role of trait and
    state envy'. *Evolutionary Psychological Science*, 9(2), 135–147.
    doi.org/10.1007/s40806-022-00344-x.

45 Borau, S & Bonnefon, JF (2019). 'The imaginary intrasexual
    competition: Advertisements featuring provocative female models
    trigger women to engage in indirect aggression'. *Journal of Business
    Ethics*, 157(1), 45–63. doi.org/10.1007/s10551-017-3643-y.

46 Arnocky, S, Davis, AC & Vaillancourt, T (2023). 'Resource scarcity
    predicts women's intrasexual competition: The role of trait and
    state envy'. *Evolutionary Psychological Science*, 9(2), 135–147.
    doi.org/10.1007/s40806-022-00344-x.

47 Bleske-Rechek, A & Lighthall, M (2010). 'Attractiveness and rivalry
    in women's friendships with women'. *Human Nature*, 21(1), 82–97.
    doi.org/10.1007/s12110-010-9081-5.

48 Baumeister, RF & Twenge, JM (2002). 'Cultural suppression of
    female sexuality'. *Review General Psychology*, 6, 166–203.

49 Vaillancourt T, Sharma A (2011). 'Intolerance of sexy peers:
    Intrasexual competition among women'. *Aggressive Behavior*,
    37(6):569–77. doi: 10.1002/ab.20413.

50 'Xena army recruit in Aust defence force' (2019) *Sunday Herald Sun*,
    26 May. Available at: ausxip.com/xena/2019/05/xena-army-recruit-
    in-aust-defence-force---sunday-herald-sun-26-may-2019.html

51 ausxip.com/xena/2019/05/xena-army-recruit-in-aust-defence-force---
    sunday-herald-sun-26-may-2019.html

52   Warner, B (2020). *Understanding Female Bullies through the Perception of Their Female Targets: A Qualitative Research Study*, ProQuest Dissertations & Theses.

53   Mavin, S & Yusupova, M (2020). 'Gendered experiences of leading and managing through COVID-19: Patriarchy and precarity'. *Gender in Management*, 35(7/8), 737–744. doi.org/10.1108/GM-09-2020-0274.

54   Hewlett, SA, Peraino, K, Sherbin, L & Sumberg, K (2011). 'The sponsor effect: Breaking through the last glass ceiling'. *Harvard Business Review, Research Report*, 1–85.

55   Warner, B (2020). *Understanding Female Bullies through the Perception of Their Female Targets: A Qualitative Research Study*. ProQuest Dissertations & Theses.

56   Agarwal, S (2016). 'Women bullying women (WBW) at workplace: A literature review', *Journal of Applied Management – Jidnyasa*, 8(1), 57–65. proquest.com/scholarly-journals/women-bullying-wbw-at-workplace-literature-review/docview/2137584555/se-2.

57   Namie. G (2024). *2024 WBI U.S. Workplace Bullying Survey*. Workplace Bullying Institute. Available: workplacebullying.org/wp-content/uploads/2024/10/2024-Complete-Report.pdf.

58   Warner, B (2020). *Understanding Female Bullies through the Perception of Their Female Targets: A Qualitative Research Study*. ProQuest Dissertations & Theses.

59   Duignan, B (2024). 'Gaslighting (human behaviour)'. *Britannica*. Available: britannica.com/topic/gaslighting.

60   See, for example, Gabriel, AS, Butts, MM, Yuan, Z, Rosen, RL & Sliter, MT (2018). 'Further understanding incivility in the workplace: The effects of gender, agency, and communion'. *Journal of Applied Psychology*, 103(4), 362–382. doi.org/10.1037/apl0000289; Loh, J, Khan, MI, Talukder, MJH (2023). 'To complain or not to complain: Management responses as a moderator in the relationship between workplace incivility and workplace outcomes among Australia and Singaporean targets', *Heliyon*, 9(11), e21363, doi.org/10.1016/j.heliyon.2023.e21363.

61 Chesler, P (2002). *Woman's Inhumanity to Woman*. New York: Nation Book.

62 Nandkeolyar, AK, Bagger, J & Ekkirala, S (2022). 'Damned if she does, damned if she doesn't: The interactive effects of gender and agreeableness on performance evaluation'. *Journal of Business Research*, 143, 62–71. doi.org/10.1016/j.jbusres.2022.01.066.

63 Leymann, H (1996). 'The content and development of mobbing at work'. *European Journal of Work and Organizational Psychology 5*, 165–184.

64 Farrington, DP (1993). 'Understanding and preventing bullying'. *Crime and Justice* (17) 381–458. The University of Chicago Press: Chicago.

65 Samnani, AK & Singh, P (2016). 'Workplace bullying: Considering the interaction between individual and work environment'. *Journal of Business Ethics*, 139(3), 537–549. doi.org/10.1007/s10551-015-2653-x p.56.

66 Workplace Bullying Institute (n.d.). 'Bullying as stressor'. Workplace Bullying Institute. Available: workplacebullying.org/target-health/.

67 Namie, G & Namie, R (2009). 'U.S. workplace bullying: Some basic considerations and consultation interventions'. *Consulting Psychology Journal: Practice and Research*, 61(3), 202–219.

68 Anasori, E, De Vita, G & Gürkan Küçükergin, K (2023). 'Workplace bullying, psychological distress, job performance and employee creativity: The moderating effect of psychological resilience'. *The Service Industries Journal*, 43(5–6), 336–357. doi.org/10.1080/02642069.2022.2147514.

69 Boddy, CR (2017). 'Psychopathic leadership: A case study of a corporate psychopath CEO'. *Journal of Business Ethics*, 145(1), 141–156. doi.org/10.1007/s10551-015-2908-6.

70 Landay, K, Harms, PD, Credé, M & Chen, G (2019). 'Shall we serve the dark lords? A meta-analytic review of psychopathy and leadership'. *Journal of Applied Psychology*, 104(1), 183–196. doi.org/10.1037/apl0000357.

71   Babiak, P & Hare, RD (2006). *Snakes in Suits: When Psychopaths Go to Work*. New York: Harper-Collins.

72   Kets de Vries, MFR (2012). 'The Psychopath in the C Suite: Redefining the SOB'. Working paper. Available: ketsdevries.com/author/papers/.

73   See, for example, Martínez-Ferrero, J, García-Meca, E & Ramón-Llorens, MC (2023). 'What if my boss is a narcissist? The effects of chief executive officer narcissism on female proportion in top management teams'. *Business Ethics, the Environment & Responsibility*, 32(4), 1201–1216. doi.org/10.1111/beer.12559; Pilch, I & Turska, E (2015). 'Relationships between Machiavellianism, organizational culture, and workplace bullying: Emotional abuse from the target's and the perpetrator's perspective'. *Journal of Business Ethics*, 128(1), 83–93. doi.org/10.1007/s10551-014-2081-3.

74   Edmondson, L & Zeman, LD (2009). 'Hurt people hurt people: Female bully-victims'. *Reclaiming Children and Youth*, 18(3), 24.

75   Kets de Vries, MFR (2014). 'The Psycho-path to disaster: Coping with SOB executives'. *Organisational Dynamics*, 43(1), 17–26.

76   Noor, N, Beram, S, Huat, FKC, Gengatharan, K & Mohamad Rasidi, MS (2023). 'Bias, halo effect and horn effect: A systematic literature review'. *International Journal of Academic Research in Business & Social Sciences*, 13(3). doi.org/10.6007/IJARBSS/v13-i3/16733.

77   Women's Economic Equality Taskforce, 'Current state of women's economic inequality – examining the data', *A 10-year-plan to unleash the full capacity and contribution of women to the Australian economy 2023–2033*, Commonwealth of Australia, Department of the Prime Minister and Cabinet. Available: pmc.gov.au/resources/10-year-plan/current-state.

78   Salin, D (2003). 'Bullying and organisational politics in competitive and rapidly changing work environments'. *International Journal of Management and Decision Making*, 4 (1), 35–46.

79   Geniole, SN, Keyes, AE, Mondloch, CJ, Carré, JM, McCormick, CM & Yovel, G (2012). 'Facing aggression: Cues differ for female versus male faces'. *PLoS One*, 7(1), e30366-e30366. doi.org/10.1371/journal.pone.0030366.

80   Beattie, Y (2014). 'Something in the water? In Australia, male CEOs with daughters have smaller gender pay gaps in their companies'. *Womanthology*. Available: womanthology.co.uk/something-water-australia-male-ceos-daughters-smaller-gender-pay-gaps-companies-yolanda-beattie-public-affairs-executive-manager-workplace-equality-agency.

81   Huntley, AL, Potter, L, Williamson, E, Malpass, A, Szilassy, E & Feder, G (2019). 'Help-seeking by male victims of domestic violence and abuse (DVA): A systematic review and qualitative evidence synthesis'. *BMJ Open*, 9(6), e021960-e021960. doi.org/10.1136/bmjopen-2018-021960.

82   Kellerman, B & Rhode, DL (Eds.) (2007). *Women and Leadership: The State of Play and Strategies for Change*. Jossey-Bass, a Wiley Imprint: San Francisco CA.

83   Hewlett, SA, Peraino, K, Sherbin, L & Sumberg, K (2011). 'The sponsor effect: Breaking through the last glass ceiling'. *Harvard Business Review, Research Report*, 1–85.

84   Single, L, Donald, S & Almer, E (2018). 'The relationship of advocacy and mentorship with female accountants' career success'. *Advances in Accounting*, 42, 12–21. doi.org/10.1016/j.adiac.2018.06.002.

85   Olivola, CY & Todorov, A (2010). 'Elected in 100 milliseconds: Appearance-based trait inferences and voting'. *Journal of Nonverbal Behavior*, 34(2), 83–110.

86   Gloor, J. L., Okimoto, T. and Backes-Gellner, U. (2023) 'How women on boards navigate the warmth-competence line', Harvard Business Review, January. hbr.org/2023/01/how-women-on-boards-navigate-the-warmth-competence-line

87   Schafer, J (2022). 'Make friends by increasing your likability quotient'. *Psychology Today*. Available: psychologytoday.com/intl/blog/let-their-words-do-the-talking/202206/make-friends-increasing-your-likability-quotient.

88   Fox, C. (2024). *Breaking the Boss Bias: How to Get More Women into Leadership*. New South Books. Sydney, NSW.

89   de Waal, F (1989). *Peacemaking among Primates*. Cambridge: Harvard Business Review Press.

90   Chira, S (2017). 'Why women aren't C.E.O.s, according to women who almost were'. *The New York Times*. Available: nytimes.com/2017/07/21/sunday-review/women-ceos-glass-ceiling.

VANESSA VERSHAW RUNS A GLOBAL ADVISORY SPECIALISING IN LEADERSHIP, CULTURE AND STRATEGY

Vanessa Vershaw is an award-winning high-performance coach and workplace psychologist who helps leaders and organisations achieve extraordinary results through mindset transformation and strategic reinvention. A trusted advisor to ASX-20 and Fortune 100 companies, she has spent over two decades guiding top executives to navigate complexity, build adaptive cultures, and unlock leadership potential.

Her expertise spans rapid business reinvention, leadership succession, high-impact team transformation, and creating adaptive, people-centred cultures. **She helps leaders break through limits, drive innovation, and cultivate workplaces where performance and wellbeing thrive.**

With a background in business psychology, neuroscience, and design thinking, Vanessa blends cutting-edge research with real-world strategy to drive lasting impact. She is a sought-after speaker, author, and media commentator, regularly featured on national television and radio discussing leadership, transformation, and the future of work.

Beyond her work, her most significant achievement is as a proud mother of two. Vanessa loves to travel, cross-country ski, box, run and write. She's inspired by the arts, random acts of kindness, and people whose souls are impatient to evolve

need more
OF VANESSA IN YOUR LIFE?

Want some more Vanessa Vershaw in your life?

If this book has been a gamechanger for you, there are a number of ways you can work with Vanessa.

Read on and head to her website vanessavershaw.dcom for more information. Follow her on Linkedin, Instagram, and Facebook for conversations and articles around the topics that matter.

WHO DO YOU KNOW THAT NEEDS THIS BOOK?

The perfect gift for clients, teams and colleagues – give *The Sisterhood Paradox* to the leaders, big thinkers and creative dreamers in your life.

Reach out to hello@vanessavershaw.com to discuss the options for bulk orders and personalised gifts for your upcoming events.

VALKYRIE
Coaching Program

Not all coaches are created equal – especially when it comes to bold, ambitious women.

Vanessa Vershaw is on a mission to ignite fearless leadership and empower women to step into their full potential–personally and professionally.

She doesn't just coach; she activates transformation, equipping female leaders with the mindset, strategies, and confidence to shatter ceilings and rewrite the rules of success.

With a powerhouse blend of high-performance coaching, psychology, neuroscience, and personal transformation, Vanessa has guided leaders across ASX-20 and Fortune 100 companies to embrace bold moves and accelerate their impact.

This is more than coaching–it's a revolution in leadership.

Are you ready to step up and claim your place at the table?

 Vanessa works with a select number of individuals and teams each year, learn more about the Valkyrie program at vanessavershaw.com/valkyrie-coaching.

To discuss bespoke and ongoing coaching packages, please email hello@vanessavershaw.com.

TRAILBLAZER

The Key to Advancing Organisations with Strong Female Leadership

Trail-Blazer is an award-winning program designed to empower female changemakers to step into their full potential and lead with purpose. Grounded in evidence-based psychological principles and adult learning science, the program drives key shifts in leadership:

Mind Shift: Building resilience, embracing uncertainty, and leading with purpose to unlock full potential.

Skill Shift: Enhancing critical thinking, creative problem-solving, and effective communication for impactful leadership.

Behaviour Shift: Leading authentically, developing empathy, and inspiring others with a visionary approach.

Systems Shift: Cultivating awareness, building leadership networks, and fostering inclusive cultures for sustainable success.

Trail-Blazer equips leaders to thrive and drive change, creating a lasting impact.

 Vanessa works with a select number of organisations each year, to find out more getting Trail-Blazer into your workplace, please email hello@vanessavershaw.com.

SPEAKING

"Engaging, insightful, mesmerising, fascinating, challenging, intoxicating, captivating."

Need a dynamic, highly experienced world class speaker for your next live or virtual event?

Vanessa is frequently sought out to motivate, inspire and deliver thought leadership to some of the most respected companies in the world.

Vanessa is a renowned authority on the following related topics;

- Open Your Kimono and Lead With Who You Are not What You Know
- Turning Setbacks into Stepping Stones for Career Success
- Harnessing Inclusive Leadership to Drive Business Growth
- Shut the Duck Up and Own Your Success

And her celebrated keynote - Talking About Sex; Leverage the Magic That Diversity Brings

 Download Speaker Kit at vanessavershaw.com/speaker-kit and then reach out to the team to discuss your next event at hello@vanessavershaw.com.au.

INTERVIEW VANESSA

A former budding Journalist with the ABC, her media features include Channel 7, 10 as well as regular appearance on Channel 9 as a Workplace Psychologist. Vanessa is also a regular on national radio covering topics around future of work, diversity, inclusion, leadership, business psychology, transformation, and world issues.

She has been published and featured in The Australian, Financial Review; Diplomat Magazine, The Globe and Mail, The Ottawa Citizen, Ottawa Business Journal, WA Business News and Emergent Magazine to name but a few.

 If you would like to interview Vanessa about her latest book, *The Sisterhood Paradox*, or any of the topics above please email hello@vanessavershaw.com. Vanessa also loves participating as part of a panel.

more to read

UNREASONABLE AMBITION

Renegade thinking for leaders to create impossible change

We are at the edge of a new frontier of business leadership which can feel like a permanent rollercoaster ride of constant change and disruption and no one is immune to these forces. Adapting to the new logic of business competition means creating opportunities from uncertainty and being witness to extreme reactions at both ends of the spectrum. Some leaders are energised by the adventure of what lies ahead, others are straining under the burden of confronting a future that is largely unchartered, with no rulebook or guardrails. Leaders who are able to channel their renegade thinking and create impossible change will be the ones to bend the world to their vision for a brighter future, they must have unreasonable ambitions for what's possible.

In her second book, *Unreasonable Ambition*, Vanessa Vershaw uses her more than 20 years of experience as a trusted advisor, strategist and high-performance coach to executive heavyweights from ASX-20 to Fortune 100 companies to share the power of having unreasonable ambition. Being unreasonable is about having a pioneering worldview. It's about thinking big and beyond and *Unreasonable Ambition* brings the two together to challenge prevailing myths about what it takes to be at your best when it matters the most.

Created as a handbook for current and emerging leaders readers will walk away with a new perspective and toolkit to face the revolutionary era we are living in.

Available on Kindle, in Paperback or Audiobook editions.